# TRAVEL WRITING

From Herodotus's *Histories* to the best-sellers of Peter Mattheissen, travel literature has attracted a wide readership since ancient times. This unique form of nonfiction, with origins in classical Greece, includes journals, diaries, memoirs, and ships' logs, as well as narratives of exploration, adventure, and escape, which seek to document encounters between self and other, to mediate between the familiar and the foreign. Casey Blanton surveys the genre's development from classical times to the present, with an emphasis on Anglo-American travel writing since the eighteenth century. Identifying significant theoretical and critical contributions to the field, Blanton presents an engaging historical overview of travel writing and provides close readings of exemplary texts by six major figures: James Boswell, Mary Kingsley, Graham Greene, Peter Matthiessen, V. S. Naipaul, and Bruce Chatwin. The first study of the genre to combine synthesis and analysis at a level accessible to students, scholars, and general readers, *Travel Writing: The Self and the World* offers an inviting supplement for course work and independent exploration.

**Casey Blanton** is Associate Professor of English at Daytona Beach Community College.

# TRAVEL WRITING

# GENRES IN CONTEXT

*Genres in Context* is an essential series of critical introductions to major literary genres. Each book in the series includes:

- A historical overview of the genre
- In-depth analysis of key texts
- A list of works for further reading
- A chronology of authors, works, and historical events
- An annotated bibliography

Books in the *Genres in Context* series include:

BIOGRAPHY
Writing Lives
Catherine N. Parke

THE FAIRY TALE
The Magic Mirror of Imagination
Steven Swann Jones

FANTASY
The Liberation of Imagination
Richard Mathews

NATURE WRITING
The Pastoral Impulse in America
Don Scheese

SCIENCE FICTION AFTER 1900
From the Steam Man to the Stars
Brooks Landon

SCIENCE FICTION BEFORE 1900
Imagination Discovers Technology
Paul K. Alkorn

THE SEA VOYAGE NARRATIVE
Robert Foulke

THE SHORT STORY
The Reality of Artifice
Charles E. May

TRAVEL WRITING
The Self and the World
Casey Blanton

# TRAVEL WRITING

## THE SELF AND THE WORLD

Casey Blanton

Routledge
Taylor & Francis Group

NEW YORK AND LONDON

Published in 2002 by
Routledge
29 West 35th Street
New York, NY 10001
www.routledge-ny.com

Published in Great Britain by
Routledge
11 New Fetter Lane
London EC4P 4EE
www.routledge.co.uk

Routledge is an imprint of the Taylor and Francis Group.
Printed in the United States of America on acid-free paper.

First Routledge paperback edition 2002.

Originally published in hardcover by Twayne Publishers, an imprint of The Gale Group.
This paperback edition published by arrangement with Twayne Publishers.

10 9 8 7 6 5 4 3 2 1

Library of Congress Cataloging-in-Publication Data

Blanton, Casey.
    Travel writing : the self and the world / by Casey Blanton.
        p. cm. — (Genres in context)
    Includes bibliographical references and index.
    ISBN 0-415-93893-7 (pbk. : alk. paper)
    1. Travelers' writings, English—History and criticism. 2. Travelers' writings,
American—History and criticism. 3. American Prose literature—History and
criticism. 4. English prose literature—History and criticism. 5. Authorship—
Psychological aspects. 6. Travel—Psychological aspects. 7. Travel writing—
History. 8. Self in literature. I. Title. II. Series.

PR756.T72 B57 2002
820.9'355—dc21                                                          2002026719

For Eli

# Contents

# Chapter 8

# Preface

In some ways, this study of travel writing has been a Sisyphean task. Just when I thought I had organized the material into a manageable bulk, word would come of a long-out-of-print book by a man crossing the Sahara, west to east, alone, or of the translated journals of the Dakar-Djibouti Mission. The texts, in the end, seemed inexhaustible. In addition to the sheer number of travel books, there was also a problem of scope and definition. Do Annie Dillard's "travels" at Tinker Creek, like Thoreau's excursions at Walden Pond, qualify as travel writing? Does Spalding Gray's *Swimming to Cambodia* qualify? "Writings of Place," it would seem, encompassed a surprisingly wide range of nonfiction works. Once I understood, however, that travel books are vehicles whose main purpose is to introduce us to the other, and that typically they dramatized an engagement between self and world, it was a matter of focusing on the various ways the observing self and the foreign world reverberate within each work. It made sense, then, to emphasize exemplary models rather than hope for exhaustive coverage.

In defining the genre we call travel literature, my purpose was to identify both individual contributions and to trace the evolution of the genre. Often this strategy was at cross-purposes, because while the modern travel book can and does avail itself of countless past models, seeming never to have evolved at all, in significant ways there can be a claim for evolution and change within that genre. The change comes, I argue, at the nexus of the narrator's sense of him or herself as creator of a text and of the involvement with the other (as persons, places, and moral and aesthetic universes) about whom the text is written. As always, there is the danger of drawing too neat an evolutionary pattern, of using broad inclusionary terms, and inevitably leaving out the "little histories." Identifying patterns in history is always risky because of the importance of context and interpretation; rivers and those who step into them are always in flux.

These caveats aside, my purpose remained to define the genre of travel writing by means of sketching its long and complex history considered largely as a function of changes in the nature of the narrator's place in the narrative. This foregrounding of the narrator is central to an understanding of the travel book, especially when one wants to account for differences between older and more recent models. To that end, chapter 1 traces the issue of self and other in travel writing ranging from the ancient Greeks to the so-called post-tourism books of today. While doing so, I suggest that the social, political, and philosophical forces that helped cause travel writing to change continue to exert pressure on the relationship between selves and the worlds they inhabit and explore.

Having defined and accounted for what a travel book is, the task of choosing some representative authors and texts was the next and, in some ways, biggest challenge. Besides accounting for and exhibiting the patterns of development in the genre, I also wanted to examine the most important practitioners of the genre, by doing close readings of their texts. While it was clear that James Boswell and his hypersensitive 1760s Grand Tour journals indicated a beginning of the travel book as I had defined it, it was less clear who would follow him, or rather who would be eliminated because of constraints on length. A historical sampling determined that I should attempt to analyze at least one travel writer from the eighteenth, nineteenth, and twentieth centuries. James Boswell in the eighteenth century and Mary Kingsley in the nineteenth century both seemed to fit my criteria of literary travel writers who spoke for themselves as well as for the issues of their day. I could have spent more time, especially in the nineteenth century, with travel writers such as Isabella Bird, Alexandra David-Neel, Charles Dickens, Robert Louis Stevenson, or any number of others who were daring, literate, and significant to the genre. Yet, because the travel book as it exists today is peculiarly modern and can never return to the rather innocent days of the Grand Tour or of colonialist journeys, I sensed that it was important to focus on the giants of the twentieth-century travel book as a way to suggest what had become of the travel book and where it might be headed in the twenty-first century.

To that end, I began the twentieth-century analysis with the so-called heyday of travel literature, the period between World Wars I and II. That so many established writers including Robert Byron, Freya Stark, Rebecca West, Peter Fleming, and Evelyn Waugh were also traveling and producing remarkable travel books, made the representation of this era by one or two writers especially difficult. Graham Greene seems particularly representative of this period because of his tendency toward psychological travel and literary models. Moving forward from that period into the mid-century was equally challenging. It would be hard to ignore V. S. Naipaul, and he takes a central place in the post-colonial period, but the inclusion of Peter Matthiessen, often considered a nature writer or a polemicist, was more problematical. In addition to analyzing his contemporary views on the complex relationships between man and nature, I wanted to indicate by his inclusion the close links between nature and travel writing that have always existed within the genre. Finally, Bruce Chatwin was my choice as the subject of the final chapter because of the literary risks he takes and the possibilities his self-reflexiveness opens up for the genre.

Chatwin shows us that for a writer in the 1970s and 1980s, it was possible to deconstruct not only the ways in which one traveled, but also the ways in which one chose to write about it. Post–Viet Nam era travelers such as Pico Iyer, John Krich, and Jonathan Raban are more willing to go alone, on foot, and be content with "native" standards of comfort. The spirit of this period in travel and travel writing is to move in close, to listen, to talk, to wonder, because the sloughing off of received truths makes for lighter traveling. When a writer journeys with fewer norms, he can better appreciate the variety of truths the world has to offer. As John Krich says of his and Chatwin's generation of wanderers, "[we were] turning travel into science, science into myth and anthropology into the work of unearthing the present" (Krich, 236).

Recent work in anthropology and ethnology, especially the work of Clifford Geertz and James Clifford, have been key to understanding not only the ways in which the genre has changed rather dramatically in the late twentieth century, but also the ways we might begin to question travel writing's long entanglement with the other. As James Clifford asks,

> Who has the authority to speak for a group's identity or authenticity? What are the essential elements and boundaries of ethnology, travel, modern interethnic relations? What narratives of development, loss, and innovation can account for the present range of local oppositional movements? (Clifford, 8)

One answer to these questions becomes the most telling characteristic of late-twentieth-century travel literature, and the one that will undoubtedly continue into the next century. Most contemporary travel writers share a sense of themselves as exiles. And part of the darkness in their books comes from their tendency to portray a world full of exiles, or even a world exiled from itself. A search for authenticity, wholeness, and meaning often drives their journeys as it did for travel writers in the past. Yet, the understanding that authenticity is not a stable entity, but a "predicament of culture" is most often the final realization of this most recent travel writing.

So much more could have been said about these themes and their relevance to all contemporary literature. To question authenticity, meaning, and authority, after all, is the hallmark of the postmodern era. Travel writing has no special claim on these issues. Yet these concerns have always been up front in travel writing as they rarely are in fiction. The disappearance of the barrier between fact and fiction, for example, seemed to me to be an especially important area of inquiry, but one that would have taken me down another road entirely. The journey I took had self imposed limitations, but the questions raised along the way were worthy of several new beginnings.

# Chronology

| | |
|---|---|
| ca. 484 B.C.E. | Herodotus is born. |
| ca. 460–445 | Herodotus travels the Mediterranean and writes *Histories*. |
| ca. 427–408 | Herodotus dies. |
| ca. 400 C.E. | Egeria makes her trip to the Holy Land. She writes letters to fellow nuns, later to become *Peregrinatio*. |
| ca. 1254 | Marco Polo is born. |
| 1296 | Marco Polo dictates *Travels* to Rusticiano while in prison. |
| 1324 | Marco Polo dies. |
| 1451 | Christopher Columbus is born. |
| 1492 | Columbus reaches the West Indies and begins his *Journal* in the form of letters to King Ferdinand and Queen Isabella of Castile. Original lost, most of what remains is transcription of what Columbus allegedly told Bishop Bartolome de las Casas. |
| 1506 | Christopher Columbus dies. |
| ca. 1554 | Sir Walter Ralegh is born. |

1595  Ralegh travels to South America.

1596  Ralegh writes and publishes *The Discoverie of the Large, rich, and Beautiful empyre of Guiana, with a relation of the great and Golden citie of Manoa (which the Spaniards call El Dorado).*

1618  Ralegh dies.

1689  Lady Mary Wortley Montagu is born.

1716–1718  Montagu writes letters home from Turkey where she accompanied her husband, the British ambassador.

1740  James Boswell is born.

1762  Lady Mary Wortley Montagu dies.

1773  Johnson and Boswell make their famous tour of Scottish Hebrides.

1775  Johnson's *A Tour to the Western Islands of Scotland* is published.

1785  Boswell's *A Journal of a Tour to the Hebrides with Samuel Johnson* is published.

1795  Boswell dies.

1809  Charles Darwin is born.

1817  Henry David Thoreau is born.

1831  *Beagle* leaves London for a three-year scientific voyage.

1834  *Beagle* returns to London.

1837  Darwin's "diaries" are published.

1845  Darwin's *Voyage of the Beagle* is published under that name.

1849  Thoreau's *A Week on the Concord and Merrimack Rivers* is published.

1862  Thoreau dies; Mary Kingsley is born.

1882  Charles Darwin dies.

1897  Kingsley's *Travels in West Africa* is published.

1900  Mary Kingsley dies.

1903    Evelyn Waugh is born.

1904    Graham Greene is born.

1911    Paul Bowles is born.

1915    Roland Barthes is born.

1927    Peter Matthiessen is born.

1930    Waugh's *Labels* is published.

1932    V.S. Naipaul is born.

1936    Greene's *Journey without Maps* is published.

1941    Paul Theroux is born.

1942    Bruce Chatwin is born.

1957    Bowles's *Their Heads Are Green and Their Hands Are Blue* is published.

1964    Naipaul's *Area of Darkness* is published.

1966    Evelyn Waugh dies.

1977    Chatwin's *In Patagonia* is published.

1978    Matthiessen's *The Snow Leopard* is published.

1978    *The Snow Leopard* receives National Book Award.

1980    Roland Barthes dies.

1989    Bruce Chatwin dies.

1991    Graham Greene dies.

Chapter 1

# NARRATING SELF AND OTHER: A HISTORICAL OVERVIEW

Melville's Ishmael, sole survivor of an epic journey and something of a travel writer himself, discovers the central dilemma of travel literature when he begins to tell the reader of *Moby-Dick* about Queequeg's home: "It is not down on any map. True places never are."[1] Ishmael's attempts to represent the exotic island homeland of his friend are frustrated by the inherent difficulty of faithfully rendering the foreign into familiar terms. As every travel writer knows, maps and books can tell only part of the truth. By what process, using what models, does the traveler presume to describe, to interpret, to represent people and places who are other to him? What encounter is included, what person omitted? What vistas extolled, what river left behind? Despite these very real difficulties, every travel writer also knows that he or she will find a way. And the large, unruly, amorphous set of discourses we call "travel literature" is a testament to that effort.

Travel literature has a long and honorable history. Early travelers' accounts like those of Herodotus (*History of the Persian Wars*, ca. 440 B.C.E.), Strabo (*Geographica*, ca. 23 C.E.), and Pausanias

1

(*Guide to Greece,* ca. 170 C.E.) are evidence of a vigorous nascent genre. These narratives and the ones that follow them render in words the strange, the exotic, the dangerous, and the inexplicable; they convey information about geography as well as human nature; they try, as Ishmael tried, to tell a kind of truth that paradoxically may be untellable. This compelling urge to describe the journey does not diminish throughout history, and there seems to be no end to the wealth of travel texts. But, as we shall shortly see, both the purpose and the style of these narratives do evolve substantially over time. It is a kind of evolution that betrays its long ancestry because the more narrow group of narratives that we have come to call "the modern travel book" has inherited elements of all of its predecessors as well as its close cousins. This complex family, then, includes memoirs, journals, and ships' logs, as well as narratives of adventure, exploration, journey, and escape.

Despite changes in style and purpose, the effect of these narratives on the reader has not diminished. From Marco Polo to Bruce Chatwin, travelers' tales about distant places and exotic cultures have proven to be remarkably popular reading. The persistence of this kind of writing is undoubtedly related to human curiosity and to a travel writer's desire to mediate between things foreign and things familiar, to help us understand that world which is other to us. But curiosity alone does not account for the persistence of this genre.

What may go further toward explaining travel literature's longevity is its narrative power, both literal and symbolic. The travel narrative is a compelling and seductive form of storytelling. Its reader is swept along on the surface of the text by the pure forward motion of the journey while being initiated into strange and often dangerous new territory. The traveler/narrator's well-being and eventual safe homecoming become the primary tensions of the tale, the traveler's encounter with the other its chief attraction. Indeed, the journey pattern is one of the most persistent forms of all narratives—both fiction and nonfiction. Works as various as the *Odyssey, Gilgamesh, Moby-Dick,* and the travel books of Mungo Park, Gertrude Bell, and Jan Morris all follow this ancient pattern: departure, adventure, and return. Yet, these works resonate with a symbolic and psychological truth that goes beyond their compelling narrative surfaces. The transformation from a literal journey to a psychological or symbolic one may occur for a number of reasons. The shift works on an intuitive level because of what Joseph Campbell calls the existence of the "monomyth," where the hero is seen as one who travels along a path of self-improvement and integration, doing battle with the "others" who are the unresolved parts of himself or herself. Wholeness is associated with homecoming when the quest cycle is complete.[2] In her book on the journey narrative in American literature, Janis Stout suggests that the symbolic power of these tales resides in "the elemental questions of epistemology, the relation between subject and object, knower and known."[3] In an explanation similar to Campbell's, she focuses on the bifurcation of the traveling self into "considering subject and considered object" (Stout, 14) where the experiences in the outer world can be "transferred" to the self that is being scrutinized, thus converting the journey into a mode of introspection. Whether fiction or nonfiction, there exists in the journey pattern the possibility of a kind of narrative where inner and outer worlds collide. But, as a survey of the development of the genre will show, the balance of that dialogue between the mind of the traveler and the observable world has not remained constant. As the purpose of travel has shifted from political exploration or mercantile errands to travel for its own sake, gradual but fundamental changes have occurred in the narratives that describe these trips. Those changes occur at the nexus of the traveler's concern with inner and outer worlds.

At one end of the spectrum lie the object-bound journey accounts of sailors, pilgrims, and merchants whose trips were inspired by necessity or well-defined purpose: exploration, devotion, or economics. These journey narratives of early travelers usually appear as ships' logs or, more commonly, as in the case of Christopher Columbus, letters to king, sponsor, or loved ones at home. In these accounts, people and places of the outer world are described in what is taken by the narrator to be a factual, disinterested way; the narrator's thoughts and reactions are all but hidden. (This is not to say, of course, that the narrator's *purpose* is hidden as well. Even while reporting in an ostensibly factual way, most early explorers and travelers undoubtedly had political and religious agendas concerning the places they were describing. Cortés's documents to the king of Spain, for instance, while purporting to be factual accounts of his travails in Mexico, were clearly designed to curry favor and to raise more money for his adventures.) At the other end of the rather long and continuous line of travel accounts lie the more explicitly autobiographical travel books that we have come to expect today as travel literature. In the works of twentieth-century travel writers, especially ones like Graham Greene, V. S. Naipaul, and Bruce Chatwin, social and psychological issues are more important than facts about places and events. Sights and vistas may not be as central to the narrative as issues of religion, politics, and social behavior. But more important, there exists at the center of travel books like Greene's *Journey without Maps* or Naipaul's *An Area of Darkness* a mediating consciousness that monitors the journey, judges, thinks, confesses, changes, and even grows. This narrator, so central to what we have come to expect in modern travel writing, is a relatively new ingredient in travel literature, but it is one that irrevocably changed the genre.

These two types—neither pure as we shall soon see—adopt different narrative strategies. The impersonal journey narratives usually have a rather flat, linear structure—flat in the sense that there is no rising and falling action, no organizing dramatic strategy. The events are reported chronologically, following the itinerary of the trip. On the other hand, a more consciously crafted work of travel literature, while usually existing within a chronological framework, often borrows from the world of fiction to establish motivation, rising and falling action, conflict, resolution, and character. These two poles exist largely only in theory. In reality, the two constantly impinge upon one another. Anyone who has read Columbus's travel accounts knows that his own personality by way of his desires and fears creeps into his representations of the New World. And even the most self-conscious autobiographical tales of travel, like those of Claude Lévi-Strauss, Lawrence Durrell, or James Fenton, rely on rather factual descriptions of people and places wholly outside the mind of the traveler. Yet, the distinctions are important. Genuine "travel literature," as opposed to what has been called "pretravel," depends upon a certain self-consciousness on the part of the narrator that was not seized upon until after the Renaissance and, in fact, not highly developed until the concern with "sensibility" in the eighteenth century.[4]

What we have come to expect today as travel literature contains a balance of these two elements: impersonal and personal. "Successful travel literature," says Paul Fussell in his anthology about the subject, "mediates between two poles: the individual physical things it describes, on the one hand, and the larger theme that it is 'about' on the other" (Fussell 1987, 126). What travel books are "about" is the interplay between observer and observed, between a traveler's own philosophical biases and preconceptions and the tests those ideas and prejudices endure as a result of the journey. The reverberations between observer and observed, between self and world, allow the writer to celebrate the local while contemplating the universal. To catch the spirit of the genre of travel literature, then, is to isolate these later, post-Enlightenment narratives into a recognizable group with certain characteristics. Among the chief characteristics are a narrator/traveler who travels for the sake of travel itself; a narrative style that borrows from fiction in its use of rising and falling action, character, and setting; a conscious commitment to represent the strange and exotic in ways that both familiarize and distance the foreign; a writerly concern with language and literature; and finally, thematic concerns that go beyond descriptions of people and places visited. Perhaps travel writer and novelist Norman Douglas says it best.

> [T]he reader of a good travel book is entitled not only to an exterior voyage, to descriptions of scenery and so forth, but to an interior, a sentimental or temperamental voyage, which takes place side by side with that outer one, . . . the ideal book of this kind offers us, indeed, a triple opportunity of exploration—abroad, into the author's brain, and into our own. The writer should therefore possess a brain worth exploring; some philosophy of life . . . and the courage to proclaim it and put it to the test. (Quoted in Fussell 1987, 15)

Despite these very real distinctions, the latter "genuine" travel books owe much to their predecessors. Travel writing as a genre has, as we have seen, a complex, impure heritage. Many of the elements that constitute a generic description of travel literature in its final form can also be located in embryonic form in these early works of "pretravel." And, as a survey of the history of travel writing will show, the evolution of the genre produced some giants in whose shadows the modern travel writer must journey and write.

In the earliest travel writing, the physical world newly discovered was more compelling than the mind of the traveler, and the narrator's purpose was to record the details of this often exciting journey. The travelogues of early explorers and historians for the most part reveal exotic sights and strange customs. In his *Histories*, the fifth-century (B.C.E.) Greek traveler, Herodotus, shows a zest for the exotic, balanced with a historian's temper for verification and fairness. It is crucial for Herodotus to observe Egyptian animal sacrifices himself, for instance, rather than depend upon other travelers' tales for their existence. "Now, I believe these statements about Egypt and those who make them, as I myself am finally convinced that they are so, because I have seen Egypt."[5]

Yet, despite the obvious importance of Herodotus as "the father of history," he may not be, as some claim, the first travel writer. Mary B. Campbell makes a good case for the European writer Egeria as the first true travel writer.[6] As a nun from Southern Europe, Egeria's fifth-century (C.E.) journey takes the form of a pilgrimage to the Holy Land. What remains of her letter to her fellow nuns revels a direct link with travel writing today that Herodotus's *Histories* does not. While Herodotus did in fact travel, and while he did narrate in the first person, there is little sense of an organizing principle in his *Histories* aside from his desire to explain the origins of the Greek and Persian wars. Places are listed almost randomly; there is no sense of a person taking the trip on whom the reader can rely for a sense of place. Egeria's organization of her trip, though clearly a self-effacing effort, nonetheless shows the hand of a traveler going from place to place and interpreting (albeit as stations of the cross) events and sights.

> Then I remembered that according to the Bible it was near Salim that holy John baptized Aenon. So I asked if it was far away. "There it is," said the holy presbyter, "two hundred yards away." Thanking him I asked him to take us, and we set off. He led us along a well-kept valley to a very neat apple-orchard, and there in the middle of it he showed us a good clean spring of water which flowed in a single stream. There was kind of pool in front of the spring at which it appears holy John Baptist administered baptism.[7]

In this passage, one senses the mind of a traveler guiding us not only with her sense of the symbolic importance of the landscape but also with some attention to the physical details of the landscape, so different from that of her home. The inclusion of interrogation and quoted language, so rare in early travel accounts, places Egeria squarely in the center of the narrative as the inquiring, curious traveler. Yet this letter marks only a beginning in the long road toward the modern travel book. Clearly the sights of the holy land are iconographic for Egeria. The people who live there are unimportant since, for her, the pilgrimage is a trip back in sacred time. Likewise for Herodotus, the places and people he meets are generally important as living verifications of widely known stories and early histories. For both writers, the plot of their narrative is essentially given rather than invented.

By the thirteenth century, travelers—mostly missionaries and merchants—pushed the frontiers of geographical knowledge past the Holy Land to include the Far East. This period is framed by two intrepid Western travelers: Marco Polo and Christopher Columbus. Both men were determined to travel to the East far beyond their Italian home ports, Polo as a diplomat and Columbus as a government-sponsored explorer. Both offered the world narratives of their voyages, and between these two widely different accounts of the "East," fairly dramatic changes begin to occur in terms of narratives that dare to present a new world. In his *Travels* (ca. 1299), Marco Polo promises "many remarkable and extraordinary things" and he does not disappoint the reader. His book, written after his travels with the help of a ghostwriter, is full of the wonders and grotesque beings that his world had come to expect from the mysterious East. Of the inhabitants of Zanzibar he reports:

> They are quite black and go about completely naked but for a loincloth. Their hair is so curly that they can only comb it when it is wet. They have wide mouths and turned-up noses. Their eyes and lips are so protuberant that they are a horrible sight. Anyone meeting them in another country would mistake them for devils.[8]

This description, emphasizing the otherness of the natives of Zanzibar—their revolting non-Western appearance—easily leads Polo to associate them with demons. It is a good example of the tendency of all travelers until very recently to carry with them the unexamined values and norms of their own culture and to judge foreign cultures in light of those habits of belief, thus establishing a kind of control over them. But Marco Polo's *Travels* is a product of its time and as such reflects the safely ordered cosmos of medieval Europe where new information was required to dovetail somehow with scientific and ecclesiastical assumptions. While purporting to write a book for the benefit of those Europeans who could not see the wide world with their own eyes, Marco Polo merely confirms his readers' terror and resistance to wilderness and supports their own world view. While much of *Travels* is written in the first person, both plural and singular, the extent to which the personality of the narrator emerges is minimal. His "I" is another medieval authority, and Polo is like an overbearing guide pointing here and there at the things he sees, pushing the reader along with his very direct, utilitarian prose.

Marco Polo's assumptions that the other is a demon or beast is a prelude to the long and complicated history of aggression upon indigenous peoples that characterizes the works and acts of Western Renaissance explorers.[9] Christopher Columbus's own records of his four voyages to the New World, written as letters to his king and sponsor, reveal that he both exoticized the natives' strange ways and their beautiful islands and assessed them as his property. The timidity of the Arawak "Indians" who inhabit the islands he first reaches makes them easy prey for Columbus's men.

> These people have little knowledge of fighting, as Your Majesties will see from the seven I have captured to take away with us so as to teach them our language and return them, unless Your Majestie's orders are that they all be taken to Spain or held captive on the island itself. . . . Near the islet I have described there are groves of the most beautiful trees I ever saw; so green, with their leaves like those in Castile in April and May.[10]

Columbus's willingness to export natives from their homeland is well documented.[11] Indeed one can argue that despite this personal voice, so attuned to the trees of the islands, the residual effects of Columbus's experiences there are minimal. In his encounter with the other that is the West Indies, Columbus remains largely unscathed and unchanged. It is the other that is subsumed by his great mission. Renaming all the islands of the Caribbean for his own saints, Columbus makes the exotic his own.

Mary Campbell argues convincingly that this cultural and personal egotism was at the root of Columbus's contribution to the development of travel literature (M. Campbell, 209). Both his exoticizing of the natives and their island *and* his assumption of dominion over them may be related to his sense of himself as a romance hero: New World discovery as Grail Quest. Unlike Egeria who sanctifies everything she sees, or Polo who materializes everything he sees, Columbus responds to the beauty of his new surroundings while at the same time assessing these surroundings as his (or his sponsor's) property. As romance hero, he can be at once sensitive and possessive since that is the nature of a knight errant in search of the Holy Grail. What matters for travel literature is the sense we get in Columbus's letters, and not in Polo's *Travels*, of an intense personal experience mediating our response to his New World. The narrator becomes a character whose responses we can feel, made more urgent by the use of the personal pronoun "I." There is something bittersweet in all of this, however. As Campbell says, these new elements we now recognize as essential to the rise of the true travel book bear the taint of original sin. "It was in the self-love of conquering heroes that the travel memoir was born" (M. Campbell, 209).

The sixteenth and seventeenth centuries saw thousands of Europeans as "conquering heroes" traveling to and exploring the newly discovered regions of the world. This New World held special fascination. Rumors of its riches inspired the greedy; tales of a beautiful and bountiful land brought settlers; promises of freedom sent the oppressed on their own journey into the wilderness. Although most of the Western travelers' narrations recorded in Hakluyt's *Voyages* and elsewhere retain an anonymous, logbook flavor, the emergence of a personal voice, conscious of changes and emotions wrought by encounters with the foreign world, can be discerned in some of these accounts. The consistent use of this voice is a slow but steady phenomenon throughout Renaissance travel accounts.

The search for the fabled cities of gold in the New World during this time sent explorers and mercenaries like Cortés and Ralegh to search for their source. In Bernal Diaz's account of Cortés's foray into Mexico and his brutality concerning the

Aztecs, little more is revealed than a single-minded pursuit of the gold.[12] However, in Sir Walter Ralegh's account of his trip to Guiana in search of El Dorado we see a much different narrative consciousness at work.

Ralegh's approach to writing about his trip was undoubtedly inspired by the futility of his venture. His "discovery of Guiana" was in fact no more than an aborted boat ride only a few miles past the mouth of the Orinoco River, perhaps as far as the banks of the territory known as Guiana. El Dorado, chiefly a New World romance inspired by memories and fantasies of native Meso-Americans, was never reached. No stranger to literature, Ralegh consciously fashions a fictionlike narrative of this journey. He withholds the failure of his quest until the end while recounting in detail the history of the search for El Dorado at the beginning. This technique creates a certain amount of tension and at the same time elevates his quest to almost mythic status. Once he begins the story proper, he compresses events; he expands humanistic detail and seems to have a sense of the colonial intrigues that would please his readers. But above all else he fashions himself as the hero of his tale, not only as its organizing principle but also as its spiritual center. As Mary Campbell rightly suggests, Ralegh portrays himself as a kind of romance hero out of Spenser, a knight who would deliver the natives from the hands of the Spaniards (and would be equally willing to appropriate their gold).

> I made them understand that I was the servant of a queen . . . and a virgin . . . , that she was an enemy to the Castellans in respect of their tyranny and oppression . . . ; and having freed all the coast of the northern world from their servitude, had sent me to free them also and to defend the country of Guiana from their invasion and conquest.[13]

This gallant knight establishes an English foothold in Trinidad (at the expense of the Spanish already there) and sails off for Guiana, trying to find an entry way into the vast and flooded Orinoco River. He is eventually forced back into the bay and on to Trinidad. But his story does not end with the failure to reach El Dorado. His tale ends with more stories about the riches and treasures to be found, as if all the deaths and failures had been worth it. Because he brings back no descriptions of El Dorado and barely any of Guiana, Ralegh must have felt the need to bring back this well-crafted tale that celebrated not only the land and the people he met but himself as well. And *Discovery of Guiana* is just that. It has none of the tedium of other captain's reports. It has purpose, danger, adventure, failure, and new possibilities. And it has a hero, albeit mostly fictional.

This kind of travel writing, which one sees occasionally in the Renaissance, clearly opens the door for a more literary kind of book about a traveler's journey. As critic William Spengemann says, it is at this time that there is a change "in the apparent subject of the narrative from the things seen to the person seeing them, and . . . a movement of the narrator toward the experiential center of his narrative."[14] It is in the late Renaissance that travel writing finds itself with roughly two types of narratives: the logbooks and journals of sailors and explorers collected avidly by Haklyut and others for a reading public eager to have them, and these newer works whose narrator comes unabashedly to the forefront of his own tale. Both types of narratives—the scientific and the sentimental—would eventually become the two dominant models for the travel genre. It is worth pausing to discover where and why these two models become so firmly established.

By the eighteenth century the entanglement between self and world was one of the central concerns of travel writers. The influence of Locke's *Essay Concerning Human Understanding* (1690), which argued that the stimuli in the external world were crucial to the development of one's intellectual powers, is undeniable. Travel assured a constant panoply of new stimuli, hence the necessity for the Grand Tour as a kind of finishing school for university students and writers. One should add to this assessment the effects of the empiricism of Newton and his emphasis on experience and deduction as valid modes of knowing. Both Locke and Newton owe their theories to Descartes, of course, who first cracked apart "mind" and "body." His ideas about the separation of mind and matter and the ability to think of oneself as a reasoning entity (the result of one's own inward journey) created a climate in which travel writing could come of age. A narrative that combined inner and outer voyage was not only possible but even predictable. This shift has two consequences for travel writing: the emotions, thoughts, and personal quirks of the narrator become more accessible and more dominant within the narrative and the world itself, its plants, animals, and people, also become a source of knowledge for their own sake.

Johannes Fabian in *Time and the Other* suggests that this concern with collecting knowledge for its own sake about foreign people and places was a result of the "secularization of time."[15] Once time lost its sacred bearings, which awarded local specificity and context to a given area (Fabian, 2), as we saw in Egeria's travel writing, time became secular and universal. Without time's connection to regional religions, it could be awarded universal, historical, and political value for the traveler. Fabian argues that the unconscious assumptions that older is primitive and deficient, while newer is European, technologically advanced, and better, were a result of this post-Enlightenment shift.

> [N]ow, secular travel was from the centers of learning and power to places where man was to find nothing but himself. . . . [T]he idea of travel as science . . . was definitively established toward the end of the eighteenth century. (Fabian, 6)

As Mary Louise Pratt points out in her book *Imperial Eyes*, two significant events occurred in 1735 that also changed the ways in which travel and travel narratives were conceived and written.[16] One was the publication of Carl Linné's *Systema Naturae*, a system to classify all plants and animals on the planet; the second was the launching of the first international scientific expedition to determine the shape of the earth. Both events, like the use of a European concept of time, assumed that the world was in some way (usually European, bourgeois, and male) measurable, orderable, and knowable. This confidence in knowing/naming the world by scientific means, beginning in the eighteenth century, became firmly ingrained in the representations of foreign peoples and places. And, as both Fabian and Pratt point out, the effect was the production of largely Eurocentric travel narratives whose purpose is to objectively describe a foreign world. In effect, the eighteenth-century traveler begins to admit to and exploit the connection between world and self, yet the "hegemonic reflex" (Pratt 1992, 15) posits the European, and therefore modern, world as superior both in time and space. Nonetheless, this scientific, information-based travel writing would ultimately provide the major model for later practitioners of the genre.

Another result of these rather significant changes during the latter half of the eighteenth century—one we have seen hints of even as early as Columbus and Ralegh—was the kind of writing that foregrounds the narrator in an attempt to sentimentalize and/or glorify the narrator's experiences in hostile environments. Here the inner world is stressed over the outer world. A traveler's thoughts, reactions, and adventures are of paramount importance; the "scientific" descriptions of the foreign land become background for the narrator's own story. Throughout the eighteenth century these two types of travel accounts—the scientific and the sentimental—not only constitute the chief paradigms by which the foreign world is represented in writing but, more importantly for the genre, also find ways to impinge upon one another.

Even in an early eighteenth-century travel account by Lady Mary Wortley Montagu, at times an extremely sympathetic traveler, at times extremely Eurocentric, we observe not only her own spunky personality but also her concern with the customs and, for her, positive attributes of Turkish women. In a letter to her sister, dated April 1, 1717, Montagu tells of her visit to a Turkish bath. Dressed as she is in a riding habit, she nonetheless is surprised to feel no resentment, no "impertinent curiosity."

> I know no European court where the ladies would have behaved themselves in so polite a manner to a stranger. I believe in the whole there were two hundred women, and yet none of those disdainful smiles, or satirical whispers that never fail in our assemblies when anybody appears that is not dressed exactly in the fashion."[17]

Even though she knows her readers would relish "a few surprising customs of my own invention" (Montagu, 72), Montagu is faithful to her own experiences and sure enough of her own powers of observation to take on the other travel writers who had come before her. In a comparison between the romantic intrigues of the Turkish upper class and those of the English, Lady Mary surmises: "Thus, you see, dear sister, the manners of mankind do not differ so widely as our voyage writers would make us believe" (72). Even as early as 1717, Montagu is clearly interested in the customs and manners of the Turkish women. She is also concerned with foregrounding herself as travel-writer-among-travel-writers and with presenting herself as a sensitive, knowledgeable narrator.

This kind of sensitivity to the customs and feelings of foreigners becomes the focal point of a literary dispute between Tobias Smollett and Laurence Sterne. Smollett's cranky book, *Travels through France and Italy* (1766), full of complaints about foreign customs everywhere, angered Sterne who believed that a travel book ought "to teach us to love the world and our fellow creatures better than we do."[18] Sterne wanted his book to "show that the value of travelling was not in stunning adventures or exquisite views exquisitely rendered back into prose; it was, instead, in the traveler's receptivity to feelings." (Sterne, 11). Sterne meant the feelings of other people, exotic and foreign, and his thinly disguised autobiographical travel book, *A Sentimental Journey* (1768), is a testament to the "traveler's receptivity to feelings" and to his own (ironic) abilities as a "Sentimental Traveler." Neither side of this argument triumphs. Travel writing after the eighteenth century becomes stylistically and thematically marked by the ways in which writers navigate the adventures, the sights, and their own feelings. As Sterne himself recognizes in *A Sentimental Journey*, there are all kinds of travelers:

> Idle Travellers,
> Inquisitive Travellers,
> Lying Travellers,
> Proud Travellers,
> Vain Travellers,
> Splenetic Travellers.
> (Sterne, 34–35)

For the first time, in the mid to late eighteenth century, one could expect to see an obvious connection both between the personality of the traveler and his book and between the traveler and the world. James Boswell's Grand Tour journals are perhaps the best example of the ways in which travel writing was beginning to assume that both narrative and description, both traveler and world, were its subject matter and its theme.

What is interesting about the Sterne/Smollet argument is that it reveals for the first time that the travel book is accepted as a genre, even one worth arguing about. Travel and travel writing, more accepted and more readily available, had become entrenched in the European mind. Indeed by the eighteenth century many established writers had either produced travel books, or had used travel as a major structural motif in their work. Samuel Johnson, Boswell, Daniel Defoe, and Smollett all chose to convert their experiences on the Grand Tour into a travel book. Those who stayed closer to home, like Alexander Pope and Jonathan Swift, used the occasion of travel as a subject of satire in, for instance, *The Dunciad* and *Gulliver's Travels*. For the novels of Henry Fielding and Smollett a travel book–like structure enabled the picaresque heroes to move from adventure to adventure.

By the end of the century, as the precarious Enlightenment balance between science and sentiment begins to make way for the subjectivity of the romantic period, travel writing veers toward the self. The emphasis on sensitivity and feelings that a writer like Boswell exploits enables a travel writer like Mungo Park (*Travels in the Interior of Africa*, 1799) to omit all concern with scientific or anthropological observation and to render himself dramatically and sympathetically as hero of his own dangerous adventures. As a prisoner of the deep Saharan "Moors," Park is faced with the dangerous and delicate task of rebuffing the tribe's sexual curiosity about its European captive.

> The curiosity of the Moorish ladies had been very troublesome to me ever since my arrival at Benowm; and on the evening of the 25th (whether from the instigation of others, or impelled by their own ungovernable curiosity, or merely out of frolic, I cannot affirm), a party of them came into my hut, and gave me plainly to understand that the object of their visit was to ascertain, by actual inspection, whether the rite of circumcision extended to the Nazarenes, as well as to the followers of Mahomet. . . . I observed to them, that it was not customary in my country to give ocular demonstration in such cases, before so many beautiful women; but that if all of them would retire, except the young lady to whom I pointed (selecting the youngest and handsomest), I would satisfy her curiosity.[19]

Passages like these not only secured Mungo Park's reputation as a wildly popular travel writer at the end of the eighteenth century, but also served to shift the emphasis in travel writing from descriptions of people and places to accounts of the effects of people and places on the narrator. By the early nineteenth century, travel writing had clearly become a matter of self-discovery as well as a record of the discovery of others.

Armed with the notion that the world and traveler could interact via the traveler's imagination, which was a central literary concern for the romantic period as well, a whole new inspiration for traveling emerged. One no longer needed a scientific or political reason for going abroad (i.e., to seek new knowledge, complete one's education, or discover new territory). By the close of the eighteenth century, as Dennis Porter rightly observes, desire replaces duty as the motivation for travel.[20] For those who would make their travels into books, it was now possible to conceive of a consciously crafted "travel book" that could delight and please the reader with a world rendered dramatically through the traveler's often very intimate experiences.

This shift does not come without complication. By the romantic period, primarily because of the prevalence for the display of the feelings and imagination of the self, the relationship between self and world becomes complex. In her book on autobiography, Janet Gunn argues that the romantic period marked the beginning of the "full flowering of the autobiographical genre as we know it today."[21] The same claim can be made about the travel book. But neither achievement could be won without wrestling with certain problems. Gunn lays the problems faced by "self-writers" and, by extension, travel writers on the very relationship that allowed these genres to flower in the first place: the relation between self and world.

> But it is just here that there arises a set of problems in the negotiations between self and world, since the dialectic between participation and distantiation, or discovery and creation, is always in danger of being collapsed toward one side or the other: on the one side is the tendency toward idealism and the problem of the imperial self; on the other side is the tendency toward empiricism and the problem of the self's "habituation" by the world. (Gunn, 59)

Cartesian dualism haunts travel writing, and by the romantic period the tendency to include the feelings of the narrator reached its zenith, collapsing eventually toward the "imperial self."

A good example of this kind of writing is that of William Bartram, an Englishman who traveled to, among other places, the American South. Like many of the romantic writers who embraced Rousseau's concept of the nobility and happiness of simple people, Bartram often rendered the lives of the Native

Americans he met in terms of natural goodness. In his book about the American South, *Travels through North and South Carolina, Georgia, East and West Florida . . .* (1791), Bartram even goes farther at some points, transforming his experiences among these "savages" into a statement of belief about the moral perfection of the universe.

> Can it be denied, but that the moral principle, which directs the savages to virtuous and praiseworthy actions, is natural or innate? It is certain they have not the assistance of letters, or the means of education in the schools of philosophy, . . . therefore this moral principle must be innate, or they must be under the immediate influence and guidance of a more divine and powerful preceptor, who, on these occasions, instantly inspires them, and as with a ray of divine light, points out to them at once the dignity, propriety, and beauty of virtue.[22]

This rhapsodic travel book no doubt appealed to William Wordsworth who may have borrowed much of its phrasing for *The Prelude.*[23] But apart from the inspiration it provided to romantic poets, this kind of travel writing is deceiving. It seems on the one hand to have escaped from the xenophobia and Eurocentrism of medieval and Renaissance narratives by its sympathetic focus on the natives' capacity for virtuous action and the willingness even to learn something universal from them. It lacks the overlay of eighteenth-century wit that often drew attention to the author and away from the places visited. Yet there is nevertheless the specter of the "imperial self" in Bartram's insistence on the application of his own elevated feelings. Granted, his world view elevates Native Americans to a near god-like position, but at the same time, a clear understanding of the world is clouded by the golden glow of post-Enlightenment nobility imposed upon the "savages" by the writer himself.

The American travel writers, just now catching up with the popularity of their European counterparts, may have found a way out of this dilemma. Fifty years after Bartram, writers such as Henry David Thoreau and Walt Whitman begin to use the travel book in a new way. Perhaps because of the historical nature of the settling of America by Europeans and its close ties to travel, the tone and theme of American travel literature is different from that of its European counterparts. Indeed, the theme of travel, as many critics have noted,[24] is peculiar to American fiction. Both American fiction and the American travel narratives that influenced it share a response to the *idea* of travel as a symbolic act, heavy with promises of new life, progress, and the thrill of escape. Travel elevated to an idea, rather than a response to new surroundings, paves the way for a kind of travel writing that Americans excel in and which, in a sense, justifies the intrusion of the "imperial self" in the service of a larger goal. It is a type of writing that has as its source Whitman's notion of the "perpetual journey." For Whitman the trip itself is not as important as what the writer learns from it. The logical extension of this kind of travel is to make life a "perpetual journey," learning all the while. Whitman's urge to "know the universe itself as a road, as many roads, as roads for traveling souls," is a twist on the romantic idea of knowing through our feelings. In America, the idea of travel for the sake of exploring the feelings of the author, which more often than not led to travel books that glorified the self above the world, is exchanged for the search for transcendent knowledge as both the journey's motivation and its ultimate goal. American travel literature is almost always "about" something else, something beyond the senses of the traveler or even the world he sees.

Thoreau, like Whitman, made travel a central idea for all his work.

> A traveler. I love his title. A traveler is to be reverenced as such. His profession is the best symbol of our life. Going from—toward; it is the history of every one of us.[25]

Despite his very circumscribed area of personal travel, Thoreau made the idea of travel central to his writing and to his beliefs. His own life was in fact a quest for life's meaning, the nature of transcendent reality, and travel became a metaphor for the way he wanted to live. In this way, perhaps paradoxically but in a peculiarly American fashion, staying at home became a form of travel. His experiences at Walden Pond, Maine, and Cape Cod, as well as the trips along the rivers of New England, convinced Thoreau that as much could be learned close to home as by traversing the globe. He was not, however, totally disinterested in foreign travel. His notebooks show that he spent much time reading and copying passages from the current as well as classical travel books. His readings included David Livingstone's *Travels*, William Bartram's *Travels*, Richard Burton's African books, and Charles Darwin's *Voyage of the Beagle*. The passages he copied and the things he learned from these travel books find their way into his own more localized travel, giving his work a global flavor. In this way Thoreau could universalize his experience and make his travel writing "about" something other than sights and vistas. The opening section of *A Week on the Concord and Merrimack Rivers* (1849), for instance, becomes a celebration of "riverness."

> The Mississippi, the Ganges, and the Nile, those journeying atoms from the Rocky Mountains, the Himmaleh, and Mountains of the Moon, have a kind of personal importance in the anals of the world. . . . Rivers must have been the guides which conducted the footsteps of the first travellers.[26]

Perhaps because of this determination to view travel as a symbolic act, American mid–nineteenth-century travel writing left a generous legacy. As William Spengemann points out, "[The American romantic travel writers] had invented a method of portraying the world as the cause and symbol of the traveler's response to it, rather than as an independent reality which precedes and dictates his perceptions" (Spengemann, 67). Indeed, both European and American travel writing after the romantic period becomes resonant with the interactions between traveler and world. This complex interplay between self and world, between the empirical and the sentimental, signals the beginning of the richest period of travel writing: the late nineteenth and early twentieth centuries.

This period is often called the heyday of travel writing because of both the depth and the breadth of travel books that appeared between 1850 and 1930. The list of established writers who also published travel books during this period is enough to warrant attention: Charles Dickens, Robert Louis Stevenson, Mark Twain, William Howells, Henry James, D. H. Lawrence, Evelyn Waugh, W. H. Auden, and Graham Greene. There were many reasons for this phenomenon, not the least of which was the democratization of travel that occurred after the steamer and train became popular means of transportation. Taking advantage of both public curiosity and this new standard of comfort, Thomas Cook institutionalized travel with his packaged tours in 1841. Travel was now just dangerous and exotic enough to appeal to the bourgeois traveler. Motivation for travel in the nineteenth century became a complex issue. Travel in this period was not only a source of enjoyment but was also clearly balanced by a desire for education; in addition, travel provided an opportunity, especially for women, to escape the rigidity of Victorian society and, very often, to write exemplary travel accounts. An industry emerged to support these various needs, and travel books became a popular means of supplying the most literate with a vicarious journey.

Travel as an educational experience, not so much as a type of finishing school for the traveler but as a way to bring back information that would benefit the entire society, dominates the mood of Victorian travel books. The most famous of these "scientific travel books" was Darwin's account, *Voyage of the Beagle* (1839). Yet, what purports to be a naturalist's record of a five-year scientific voyage is, in fact, a very personal record of a man's awakening to the possibilities of firsthand experience and the resulting widening of his horizons, both literally and figuratively. Darwin's advice to travelers in the last chapter of *Voyage* reflects this humility before new knowledge.

> The map of the world ceases to be a blank: it becomes a picture full of the most varied and animated figures. Each part assumes its proper dimensions: continents are not looked at in the light of islands, or islands considered mere specks, which are, in truth, larger than many kingdoms of Europe.[27]

Just a paragraph later, however, Darwin extols the kind of moral improvement that England could bring to such a world that he, in part, opened for colonialism. Indeed the optimism of the late nineteenth century, fueled by a faith in perfectibility and personal progress, is a dominant theme in the travel books of the period. These Victorian-age travelers with their faith in firsthand observation and a willingness, at least up to a point, to be transformed by the world they explored, made excellent traveling companions for a rapidly expanding reading public whose appetite had been whetted by these enormously popular books.

This mood of optimism, however, was not to last. The horrors of the First World War altered the way many people thought about human progress. Along with the new century, the modern temper of doubt and anxiety was born. In *Abroad*, Paul Fussell's study of travel writing in the early part of the twentieth century, he analyzes the social and literary atmosphere in the years following World War I. Dominated as it was by the mood of lost illusions and lost lives, this period produced writers who seemed determined to desert their homelands. One thinks of the obvious exiles: James Joyce in Paris and Trieste, Ernest Hemingway in Paris, T. S. Eliot in London, and D. H. Lawrence everywhere but England. The English writers seem to have been particularly eager to travel after the First World War since its effects were felt so cruelly there. To these exiles, postwar England seemed dull, colorless, cold, and insular, and "abroad" would be the antidote. Fussell argues that because of this feeling of discontent and exhaustion, and because of the modern tendency for self-examination, travel becomes the dominant literary metaphor for the period.[28]

Travel writing naturally flourished in this atmosphere. In another book on this period of literary exiles, Samuel Hynes argues that travel writing begins at this point to emphasize the theme of self-discovery, producing what Hynes calls a "dual plane work with a strong realistic surface, which is yet a parable."[29] That modern parable concerns the quest for wholeness and a deep excavation for the self's scattered shards. The comfortable balance between self and world, between pleasure and duty enjoyed by late Victorian travel writers was thrown off kilter by the now insupportable idea of an essential self or a real world. The fragmentation of the self and the subsequent quest for wholeness explored in the works of Eliot, Joyce, Georges Braque, and Pablo Picasso appear in varying degrees in the travel writing of the early twentieth century.

Waugh, along with Greene and Robert Byron, established themselves as the giants of travel writing in this period by writing books that essentially questioned the norms of the fragmented modern world through irony. Waugh particularly is primarily interested in the gap between expectation and reality as he describes a world gone slightly insane. His irony depends, in general, on his exposure of a world turned upside down. He says, "The writer's only service to the disintegrated society of today is to create little independent systems of order of his own" (quoted in Fussell 1980, 171). His visit to the much ballyhooed coronation of Abyssinian leader Haile Selassie in 1930 provided rich material for the disparities he saw at work in the modern world.

> Eventually, about fourteen hours before the ceremony was due to start, numbered tickets were issued through the legations; there was plenty of room for all, except, as it happened, for the Abyssinians themselves. The rases and Court officials were provided with gilt chairs, but the local chiefs seemed to be wholly neglected; most of them remained outside, gazing wistfully at the ex-Kaiser's coach and the tall hats of the European and American visitors.[30]

Waugh's version of the coronation, like most of his travel writing, is full of these kinds of anomalies, where traditional expectations are constantly undermined by the reality of mismanaged pomp and circumstance. Fussell calls this technique "comic disillusion" (Fussell 1980, 174–202), and after the 1930s it becomes a standard feature of much British travel writing.

For Waugh and Greene and Byron it is much more than that, however. The humor of the between-the-wars travel book is dependent on an ironic vision of the modern world as disconnected and fragmented. Writers of the 1930s responded to such a world where as Northrop Frye says, "heroism and effective action are absent, disorganized or foredoomed to defeat,"[31] with what Alan Wilde in his book on irony calls "disjunctive irony."[32] The smooth polished surface of Waugh's writing is an attempt to control, at least in his prose, such a disjunctive world, while at the same time revealing it through the genre of the travel book. Yet, as Alan Wilde argues, the effort to control this fragmentation by consciousness and irony became the burden of modernism. "The self, in other words, whether or not intentionally, endows the world with all of its value and meaning; and it is the enormity of the task imposed upon it that accounts for the various modernist evasions and failures" (Wilde, 5). The best travel writing of the 1930s reflected this same "burden of subjectivity," a vision that can accurately describe the modern dilemma but can offer no solution to it. As Fussell shows in *Abroad*, as the Second World War approached, this kind of travel writing became bitter and politically aggressive. Such travel books of the late 1930s and early 1940s "which contrast with earlier examples of the genre, will seem little more than repositories, often incoherent, of exhaustion, bitterness, and rabid ideology" (Fussell 1980, 219). It is as though the smooth ironies or deep introspection cannot stand up to a world gone mad.

Waugh complained in 1945 that he did "not expect to see many travel books in the near future" (Waugh, 9). From his vantage point near the end of the "heyday" of travel writing, Waugh could not foresee the great revival of travel literature during the last few decades of the twentieth century and the writers who would try to assess a new madness afoot in the world. But he was partly right; for the next 20 years there would not be many travel books that matched the caliber of those of his generation. Nor were there many of such quality in the long history of travel writing prior to 1920. As Waugh himself says, "I went when the going was good" (Waugh, 9). Many of the themes and techniques—journey as metaphor, the unrelenting irony, and the concern with literary style—made travel writing of the 1930s a formidable literary movement and provided the next generation of travel writers with models. Travel writing had come of age but, Waugh's complaint notwithstanding, it was far from over.

The postwar years brought an end to the kind of journey so prized by Waugh and the travelers of the 1930s. Jet travel assured the emergence of mass tourism and the end of independent travel. In his book *The Tourist,* Dean MacCannell suggests that "mass leisure" also contributed to the rise of tourism and sightseeing in the 1950s.[33] MacCannell argues that this complacent decade produced the ritual of foreign travel as a search for "authenticity," for monuments that were not "banal, ugly, polluted, unidifferentiated" (MacCannell, 40). Ironically, the ultimate outcome of this passion for the foreign was to make everything the same. By the late twentieth century the Sistine Chapel would be thronged with 11,000 tourists a day, making authenticity questionable and travel a sort of required pilgrimage to the repositories of culture. The travel writers who resisted this experience and who instead sought complexity, authenticity, and new ways of seeing were those who represented the antiestablishment, writers like Jack Kerouac and Paul Bowles.

Kerouac's *On The Road* is a testament to the kind of postwar traveling that Waugh feared would supplant his own brand. "The very young, perhaps, may set out like the *Wandervögels* of the Weimar period; lean, lawless, aimless couples with rucksacks, joining the great army of men and women . . . who drift everywhere today between the barbed wire" (Waugh, 9). "Lean and lawless" and certainly no tourist, Sal Paradise drives relentlessly from East Coast to West, from the United States to Mexico, searching for an antidote to the materialism and conformity that he sees around him. The myth of the Beats invariably included the idea of a journey like Kerouac's.

> The myth follows authentic archaic lines, and goes something like this. The hero is the "angelheaded hipster." He comes of anonymous parentage, parents whom he denies in correct mythological fashion. He has received a mysterious call—to the road, the freights, the jazz-dens, the "negro streets." This is the night journey or journey underground.[34]

These outcasts traveled, as Gregory Corso says, with "two suitcases filled with despair." The trips with William Burroughs to Mexico and to Tangiers would often culminate in death or physical degradation, not in the regeneration of the traveler or his world. The quest motif in Beat travel writing does not come full circle. The heroes are like Balin, the knight of the Round Table who gets lost in the forest. Yet it is exactly this sort of travel and travel writing that offered new possibilities for the genre.

One writer who strongly influenced Kerouac and became a patron saint to the Beats is Paul Bowles. Bowles writes, as it were, from inside the forest. Having renounced all that is American, Bowles has been living in Morocco since the 1940s. His collection of travel pieces, *Their Heads Are Green and Their Hands Are Blue,* is written from the point of view of the exile. This perspective demands no other norm except authenticity, a certain pureness, which is an increasingly hard commodity to find in a world that anthropologist and travel writer Lévi-Strauss called a "monoculture."[35] The dilemma faced squarely by writers like Kerouac and Bowles is how to find otherness in a world dominated by sameness. Their solution is to go outside society's norms, even its travel norms. Travel in the developing world, far off the tourist routes of the 1950s, was left to anthropologists such as Mead and Malinowski. Like them, Bowles deliberately heads deep into the desert of North Africa where few westerners had ventured alone. Bowles's search for authenticity leads him into a sympathetic and scholarly study of the cultures he visits. He is particularly interested in the folk music of North Africa and begins an exhausting expedition across the desert to tape all the variations of the indigenous music before the Moroccan government, in the interest of progress, extinguishes it. His expedition is a solitary one, with local tribesmen as his guides. He is painfully aware of the problems of his own presence in the collecting of cultural artifacts. Yet, as an exile with few expectations of comfort or schedule, his patience and willingness to endure extreme conditions yield results.

> The solos are among the very best things in the collection. One called "Reh dial Beni bouhiya" is particularly beautiful. In a landscape of immensity and desolation it is a moving thing to come upon a lone camel driver, sitting beside his fire at night while the camels sleep, and listen for a long time to the querulous, hesitant cadences of the qubah. The music, more than any other I know, most completely expresses the essence of solitude.[36]

Bowles's writing is curiously flat; the beauty of the desert and the horrors of travel are recorded in the same dispassionate tone. In a retrospective review of his work, critic Geoffrey O'Brian describes this style and, in doing so, correctly sees Bowles's link to the darker side of MacCannell's conventional postwar culture.

> This is tourism degree zero: the exotic doesn't offer the traveler an alternative reality, since he has no reality to begin with. He travels into empty places—often relishing the boredom and desolation of the journey—as if to fully taste his own emptiness.[37]

Beat travel writing is distinguished by this attitude; it is characterized chiefly by a longing for unity and authenticity balanced, paradoxically, by an existential recognition of the absurdity of existence.

The period of travel writing that follows, with its roots firmly in the eccentric writers of the 1950s, is what Paul Fussell calls "post-tourism." These travel writers have not abandoned hope of discovering "something" out there—whether it be the daily habits of the Brazilian Indians or the roots of Aboriginal Songlines. Yet the awareness of the questionability of such exercises gives post-tourism "a tendency . . . toward annoyance, boredom, disillusion, even anger" (Fussell 1987, 755). Post-tourism coincides with another "post"—postmodernism, with all its in-your-face playfulness, reflexivity, and dark humor. These elements would complete the characteristics that we have come to expect in today's travel book.

Events of the 1960s did much to solidify the shift in cultural awareness that affected not only travel writing and anthropology but fiction as well. In her book on postmodern poetics, Linda Hutcheon summarizes this period. "The Viet Nam War created a real distrust of official 'facts' as presented by the military and the media, and in addition, the ideology of the 1960s had licensed a revolt against homogenized forms of experience."[38] These "forms of experience" represent the object-view of traditional, positivist history, where facts are facts and things are things, easily verifiable and calculable. But through the experiences of the antiwar movement and the civil rights movement, the period saw, as Hutcheon says, a rise in the "ex-centric" or those off center in our society, whose experiences were not those of the sanctioned majority and whose competing views of reality demanded attention (Hutcheon, 62).

For the late twentieth-century travel writer or anthropologist to ignore this shift in perspective is to hold out for the sacredness of facts, separate objects, and single truths and to ignore relatedness and paradox. Facts had served travel writing well over the centuries. Travelers from Herodotus to Darwin had made it their business to bring back facts and "true" stories for their readers. Yet, beginning with the self-doubts of the modern period, the efficacy of knowing the world by this method of us and them, true and false, right and wrong, is scrutinized and hotly debated. Questions about the role of the observer and the nature of representation itself, questions put to fiction at this time as well, demanded a change in all forms of reportage.

The awareness of the interconnectedness of all matter and the role of the observer/narrator in collecting data leads the contemporary travel writer to literally and metaphorically connect himself to the world, since he sees that the world is, in fact, himself. These "post–Viet Nam" travel writers, for the most part, travel alone, usually by foot or third-class conveyance, coming closer to the people among whom they travel than ever before. Freed from the essential certainties of self and other, this traveler embarks with less cultural baggage but with an inner struggle to define himself and assert his own presence among others who are even less clearly focused than himself. And in varying degrees these travel writers ultimately acknowledge the impossible task of gathering self and world into what ethnologist James Clifford calls "a stable narrative coherence."[39]

Stylistically these new books tend to "fall apart." Freed from strictly chronological, fact-driven narratives, nearly all contemporary travel writers include their own dreams and memories of childhood as well as chunks of historical data or synopses of other travel books. Self-reflexivity and instability, both as theme and style, offer the writer a way to show the effects of his or her own presence in a foreign country and to expose the arbitrariness of truth and the absence of norms.

These elements are evident in a short travel piece that is representative of serious travel writing since 1960. In "Polisario," Jeremy Harding, a British journalist, describes a trip to the disputed territory of Western Sahara which is claimed by both Morocco and the occupants of the territory itself, a group calling themselves the Polisario. Incredibly, Morocco's King Hassan began in 1980 to build an enormous wall meant to keep the Polisario strongholds from their own towns and phosphate mines in Western Sahara. Obsessed with this impossible project, a construct of brute power, Harding is determined to see the wall himself. The journey takes him to the middle of a decade-long war as lethargic and exasperating as the wall itself. As he wanders around its perimeter, Harding begins to see the wall as more than a pile of rocks in the desert.

> The great success of the wall, it struck me, was to assert its presence to such an extent that you seldom felt unseen or unaccounted for. It had imposed its own order on the desert by turning vast, homogeneous tracts of rubble into an arcane grid of concourses and pathways, some brightly lit and therefore dangerous, the others dark and apparently safe. Even when you were concealed behind the bluffs in Semara Sector, you still felt vulnerable.[40]

Back in London, Harding continues to see the wall as a metaphor for his own vulnerability and for the curiously torpid and uneventful war that the wall defines.

Later, in London, sorting through my photographs, I still felt that disturbing sense of exposure. . . . The wall waited and watched for Polisario; Polisario watched the wall. (Harding, 26)

But the theme of vulnerability reaches closer to home than Harding had imagined. Between trips to North Africa, Harding discovers his wife has fallen in love with their boarder, a German architect, another builder of walls. Both issues continue to obsess Harding: the wall and the German.

I spent hours reading about the wall, ordering my notes and, night after night, poring over my photographs on the kitchen table. I also listened out for the value of the Deutschmark on the World Service financial reports, hoping this might provide some clue about the survival of my marriage. It was hovering at 188 pfennings to the dollar. The German, a thoughtful man with a blond moustache, was clearly holding ground. (Harding, 27)

His own marriage becomes identified with battle, with "holding ground." The wall between Harding and his wife is suggested in his descriptions of the Saharan wall: "The first time I looked for the wall, I couldn't find it . . . It was said that more of the wall was being built all the time. No one knew how long it would finally be" (Harding, 21). Both walls ultimately prevail. Harding's wife leaves him and the Saharan wall continues to be built. "The wall was dangerous, undoubtedly. It was a magnificent structure of denial—the biggest monument to denial in the whole of Africa (Harding, 37)."

In the end, Harding returns to Western Sahara and identifies himself with the beleaguered Polisario guerrillas fighting a no-win battle with Morocco and her backers in France and the United States. The essay, besides exploring cultural wars and domestic crises, exhibits the refusal of the world to stand apart from the self any longer. The wall exposes and defines those around it. Harding internalizes the same wall and takes it as his own metaphor. In describing the world, Harding describes himself. Yet Harding's piece, despite these attempts at introspection and subjectivity, leaves the reader curiously unsettled. Finally we are up against a wall ourselves. Are we to feel pity for Harding? for the Polisario? for the German? Harding's flat tone and unemotional revelations about his marriage give us no help. The wall itself holds a key.

Nuruddin, who spoke several European languages, often used a French word, *la pourriture*, to introduce his most damning thesis about the wall. "If we left it alone," he used to say, "if we never went near it, the wall would crumble. It is made from desert and it will return to desert. Every hour it is being swept away." The word in English, I suggested, was decay. (Harding, 25)

The tendency of the wall to be unstable suggests something about both the form and the message of this travel piece, and perhaps about all post-tourism travel books. Just as the wall itself is an arbitrary construct—ever crumbling, ever unstable—so is every other institution in the story: Moroccan politics, marriage, and finally the narrative itself. There is no final solution to Harding's issues or the Polisario's; no insight is achieved. There is only—as the story ends—the sound of *la pourriture*, the crumbling of walls. This is writing that provides a narrative model within which paradox and inscrutability can become both a new style and a major theme.

Ultimately, by the late twentieth century, the role of travel books has changed. They are no longer our only source for the exotic; we can see that at our own gates and in our living rooms. The new travel books are not our guides to places remote; nowhere is remote anymore. They are instead metaphors of a quest for ground zero—a place where values are discovered along the way, not imported; a place where other cultures can have their say; a place where self and other can explore each other's fictions; a place that, as Ishmael warns us, "is not down on any map."

Because one of the central issues in travel reportage has always been the relationship between self and world, the development of the genre we have come to call travel literature is closely aligned with the changing role of subjectivity in other kinds of literature, especially fiction and autobiography. The genre has survived because it has changed. A closer look at six major figures of this fluid and adaptable genre will allow us to explore these changes in more detail.

Chapter 2

---

# "Vain Travelers": James Boswell and the Grand Tour

The modern travel book, I have suggested, features the following: a narrator/traveler who travels for the sake of travel; a narrative organization that owes much to fiction; a commitment to both a literary language and a personal voice; and thematic concerns of great moral and philosophic import. By the time a young James Boswell set off for his Grand Tour of Europe in 1763, travel books with these elements were just emerging from the wealth of voyage and discovery writing that had preceded them. Although one senses in Columbus's letters and in Ralegh's memoirs a hint of personal voice and deliberate narrative style, it was not until the eighteenth century that this tendency flourished. Boswell's travel books and his Journals did much to establish this highly personal travel writing as a standard fixture in the European canon of nonfiction literature.

As Dennis Porter has noted in his study of the period, desire conflicts with duty in the eighteenth-century traveler (Porter 10–11). Utilitarian motives for travel were replaced by very personal, even, as Porter argues, psychoscxual ones. Even though the Grand Tour was seen as an obligatory finishing school for the young men of powerful families, in fact, as Pope noted, the young men more often "sauntered Europe round, / And gathered every vice on Christian ground." The appeal to duty was more often than not an excuse to acquire a veneer of European manners, make business and political contacts, and experiment sexually in a more permissive society. In no traveler is this more apparent than James Boswell. For the young Scotsman, duty was what he was trying so hard to avoid: a law practice in Scotland, a wife and family, and the assumption of the responsibilities that the Auchinleck family name and estate demanded. Boswell fought against this respectable life with an ill-defined dream of making something more grand of himself. He had literary pretensions and an insatiable curiosity about people that drew him to London. In a very tangible sense, then, the young Boswell associated travel with desire. Indeed his first travel book was the *London Journal*, which contained the exploits of a young man let loose to enjoy himself in a strange city, far from home, father, and duty.

In his first week in London in the Fall of 1762, Boswell explored his heart's desires: sex, politics, and religion—the subjects that would fascinate him throughout his life.[1] Yet, for Boswell, desire can never totally replace duty. Throughout his travels, there is an antagonism between the two impulses. In each of the three areas there is an essential question of freedom or convention that obsesses Boswell. He never completely chooses one or the other. In the space of a week in London, Boswell's activities betray these often antagonistic preoccupations. In the *Journal* entry for Thursday, November 25, he relates a scene that would be repeated over and over in his Grand Tour and become a lifelong threat to his stability. Boswell walks home late at night through a park full of prostitutes and engages a woman. On this particular occasion he worries openly in his *Journal* about getting a venereal disease for lack of a condom; he brags about his "size."

> I was really unhappy for want of a woman. I thought it hard to be in such a place without them. I picked up a girl in the Strand; went into a court with intention to enjoy her in armour. But she had none. I toyed with her. She wondered at my size, and said if I ever took a girl's maidenhead, I would make her squeak.[2]

Four days before this incident, Boswell had been in church imagining himself a devoted Anglican. Three days after the episode in the park, Boswell returns to church with a more characteristic attitude.

> I went to St. James's Church and heard service and a good sermon on "By what means shall a young man learn to order his ways," in which the advantages of early piety were well displayed. What a curious, inconsistent thing is the mind of man! In the midst of divine service I was laying plans for having women, and yet I had the most sincere feelings of religion. (*London*, 53–54)

This paradox, this preoccupation of Boswell's with duty and desire and with faith and sex will also characterize his travel journals as a whole.

The world of politics also interests the young Boswell. Just a few hours before he engages the woman in the Strand, Boswell hears the king speak, is overwhelmed by his charisma, and immediately seeks an audience. "His Majesty spoke better than any man I ever heard: with dignity, delicacy, and ease. I admired him. I wished to be acquainted with him" (*London* 49). Boswell will be inexorably drawn to men of power—kings, generals, philosophers, and writers—and, against the greatest odds, obtains audiences with nearly all men of power and persuasion in Europe, including Rousseau and Voltaire. During this first week in London, then, we can see Boswell operating almost completely by desire—both physical and intellectual. For Boswell, travel was not so much a means of rounding out his education as it was a means of escape that would allow him to gratify his grandiose appetites. He traveled for the sake of going or, more precisely, for the sake of leaving.

Aside from the antiutilitarian inspiration for Boswell's travels, his actual writing is much different from the travel logs of sailors and explorers and even from the writings of earlier eighteenth-century travelers such as Addison whose books recorded primarily vistas and landmarks. Boswell is not strictly interested in a day-by-day, place-by-place objective account of his trip. Despite the fact that practically every day is accounted for in a massive writing effort, Boswell manages to shape his journals into a fictionlike story of a young, impressionable man's journey through the capitals of Europe. He is both conscious of literary style and impervious to the eighteenth-century's demands for decorum and distance. Many friends who read the journal complained of its bluntness and lack of artifice. Yet, objective observation is not the narrative stategy that suits Boswell, and he barely heeds their advice. What seems a natural inspiration for Boswell is his ability to turn what could be a very tedious journal into a rollicking picaresque novel and to offer perhaps the best of both—a work both personal and universal. He employs several "literary" techniques to do this: selective detail for the delineation of characters (including himself), the use of plotting and suspense, dialogue, and an underlying theme—the tension between duty and desire.

Because of Boswell's overriding curiosity about people, he is particularly good at portraying a wide range of characters. From Mrs. Legge, the laundress, to the valiant Corsican General Paoli, Boswell's characters are finely drawn. The discourse about Mrs. Legge serves no real purpose in Boswell's journal except, as in a novel, to establish background, setting, and mood. In nearly Dickensian fashion, Boswell first paints her in broad strokes, telling her history and her chief characteristics. Then he allows her to speak in her own voice, giving her life.

> At present we have an old woman called Mrs. Legge for a laundress. . . . she is perhaps as curious animal as has appeared in human shape. She presents a strong idea of one of the frightful witches in Macbeth; and yet the beldame boasts that she was once as handsome a girl as you could clap your eyes upon, and withal exceedingly virtuous. . . . She was a servant in many great families, and then she married for love a tall strapping fellow who died. She then owns she married Mr. Legge for money. He is a little queer creature; and . . . generally goes by the name of The Baron. . . .
>
> To give a specimen of Mrs. Legge, who is a prodigious prater. She said to Bob this morning, "Ay, ay Master Robert, you may talk. But we knows what you young men are. Just cock-sparrows. You can't stand it out. But the Baron! O Lord! the Baron is a staunch man. . . . Yes. yes, the Baron is a good man, an able man. He laid out a married woman upon the floor while he sent the maid out for a pint of porter. (*London*, 306–307)

This kind of digression serves the *Journal* well in that it diverts attention away from Boswell himself, yet retains the flavor of a book about a rake's progress, touching as it does on its author's preoccupation with sex and women. Boswell will perfect this kind of character study that can underscore his thematic material with portraits of Rousseau, Voltaire, and General Paoli.

Another way Boswell's *Journal* distinguishes itself from traditional travelogues and approaches fiction is in its use of plotting and suspense. A major source of suspense in the *London Journal* rests with Boswell's pursuit of an actress whom he calls Louisa. This dogged chase occupies Boswell for months. Nearly every day there is the question: Will Louisa grant Boswell sexual favors? Where will they go to consummate the affair? Will they be discovered? Did Boswell get gonorrhea from Louisa? How will he break off the affair? These questions and the thread of this affair run in and out of Boswell's other preoccupations in London: securing employment, meeting well-connected people, and attending the theater. Boswell also uses this affair to experiment with dialogue.

> BOSWELL: You have used me very ill. I did not deserve it. You know you said where there was no confidence, there was no breach of trust. But surely I placed some confidence in you. I am sorry I was mistaken.
> LOUISA: Sir, I will confess to you that about three years ago I was very bad. But for these fifteen months I have been quite well. I appeal to God Almighty that I am speaking true; and for these six months I have had to do with no man but yourself.
> BOSWELL: But by G-d, Madam, I have been with none but you, and here I am very bad.
> LOUISA: Well, Sir, by the solemn oath I protest that I was ignorant of it.
> BOSWELL: Madam, I wish much to believe you. But I own I cannot upon this occasion believe a miracle. (*London*, 159–60)

Boswell occasionally uses these dialogues instead of the more traditional memoir style of third-person reportage. Though not always successful because of their stilted tone, they do offer the reader a sense of storytelling instead of journal writing.

Throughout the Grand Tour, Boswell continues the threads of suspense established here in the *London Journal*. The question of whether or not Boswell will obtain his father's permission to go to Europe and then to continue the Tour creates much of the tension in the Grand Tour journals. Where Boswell will find his next sexual adventure is a subtext to the journals as a whole, which alternates between his melancholia and repentance and flights to the parks of Europe in search of a woman. Other larger questions tend to unify the journals: Will Boswell find who he is? Will his melancholia be cured? Will he resolve the ultimate paradox of freedom within convention?

The need to know himself through his interactions with a great variety of people is at the center of Boswell's travel writing. This tendency places him at the exact center of the narrative. Like a picaresque hero, Boswell the character has adventures, learns from them, and is changed. Indeed, like a novel, the narrative in these travel journals is arranged anecdotally rather than strictly chronologically; we go from story to story rather than from place to place. In addition, they are full of the kind of detail that is essential to telling a story, not merely describing a scene—people's motives, their manners, and their effect on the narrator. And at the center we find a curious, wonderfully open narrator who organizes the narrative as a way to explore his own mind and feelings. These characteristics, plus a highly developed literary style, make Boswell's accounts of his travel remarkable and produce a landmark in the history of travel writing.

But if Boswell is representative of the kind of travel that was to come, he is also highly eccentric. Quirky, self-absorbed, and a seeker of forbidden pleasures, Boswell makes an energetic but often irritating travel companion. His journals are sometimes too self-absorbed, his need to shine in reflected glory too obvious, his compulsion for sensual pleasure too sad. But ultimately we forgive the traveler all his eccentricities because his books are "about" something else. Boswell manages a daring feat: to connect his own personal obsessions with sex, religion, and politics, with the larger issues of principle vs. desire and order vs. freedom. Beginning with those escapes to London, the journals continue nearly unbroken for the rest of Boswell's life. As travel writing they are unified by these larger questions and a highly developed self-awareness. It is as though by writing and traveling Boswell could put into practice or test the issues that plagued him: duty to his father and conventions vs. his desires for the artistic and the wanton life; duty to the Anglican Church vs. a flirtation with Catholicism and Deism; and finally an attraction to monarchy vs. an intellectual dalliance with political and social freedom. In all the journals these issues loom large, especially in the travel accounts where Boswell seems to have felt freer not only to speculate about these overwhelming contradictions but to live them as well. Perhaps his friend Zélide caught the enormity of this preoccupation and the effect it was to have on Boswell when she wrote to him: "You love problems which can never be solved" (*Holland*, 357).

Boswell takes these problems with him to the two great philosophers of his day, Rousseau and Voltaire. He deliberately seeks them out on his travels as personal mentors in his hero's quest for self-awareness. He takes two issues to Rousseau: sex and politics. But there is a fair amount of suspense involved before he can do even that. By 1764 when Boswell makes his visit, Rousseau is, after all, an invalid and a recluse. For a young, unknown Scotsman to request an audience at Motiers with the great Rousseau requires either calculated social daring or mindless effrontery. As we have seen, this brash Scotsman lacks neither courage in social affairs nor sufficient ego to presume Rousseau might want to see him. In Boswell's ongoing quest for a personal audience with the prominent leaders and thinkers of Europe, he writes a letter designed to intrigue this great man and to present Boswell in his best light, that is, a curious, easy-going, intelligent young man in search of personal advice from the philosopher.

> Open your door, then, Sir, to a man who dares to tell you that he deserves to enter it. Place your confidence in a stranger who is different. You will not regret it. But I beg you, be alone. In spite of all my enthusiasms, after having written to you in this fashion, I know not if I would not prefer never to see you than to see you for the first time in company. I await your reply with impatience. (*G&S*, 215)

Despite the flattering logic, it is probably the letter's intense self-involvement that piques Rousseau's curiosity in the end and causes him to respond positively, albeit ironically: "I am ill, in pain, really in no state to receive visits. Yet I cannot deprive myself of Mr. Boswell's" (*G&S*, 215). The two meet and speak in very general terms—too general and not personal enough for Boswell. His solution is to send a long letter to Rousseau describing his personal life in order to ask more specific advice during the next meeting.

As we have seen predicted in the *London Journal*, one of Boswell's favorite and most compelling conundrums was the place of sexual freedom in a conventional society. Three weeks before Boswell is to leave on the tour of Europe, and after having met Samuel Johnson, he manages to intellectualize this dilemma.

> Since being honoured with the friendship of Mr. Johnson, I have more seriously considered the duties of morality and religion and the dignity of human nature. I have considered that promiscuous concubinage is certainly wrong. . . . Sure it is that if all the men and women in Britain were merely to consult animal gratification, society would be a most shocking scene. Nay, it would cease altogether. . . . I am now resolved to guard against it. (*London,* 304)

But, consistent with Boswell's dual nature, his memorandum for the day, which was the rough draft of his *Journal*, states, "Swear to have no more rogering before you leave England except Mrs. _____ in chambers." (*London*, 304).

No amount of resolve ever prevented Boswell from seeking pleasure with women wherever he traveled, so the issue becomes for him one of character and philosophic inquiry during the Grand Tour that begins shortly after this entry. Even while in Germany, Boswell hears gossip about Lord Baltimore who was reputed to have kept a seraglio. Boswell writes, "Lord Baltimore was a beacon to me. I trembled to think of my wild schemes." (*G&S*, 48) Three months later at Rousseau's house in Motiers, he confesses that he dreams of keeping concubines. Indeed much of Boswell's visit with Rousseau is occupied with Boswell's dilemma of happiness vs. an "evil" life. Here Boswell seems to be actively pursuing the solution of having many sexual partners and no guilt. Rousseau's answer is deceptively simple. He advises the young Boswell to follow the rules of society and to "expiate evil by doing good." In what is perhaps even better advice, Rousseau says, "Your great difficulty is that you think it so difficult a matter" (*G&S*, 252). Boswell is not entirely satisfied with the philosopher's answers. (Indeed he all but ignores the famous man, who by this time had become an alternative father figure, when later on a train he seduces Rousseau's mistress, Thèrése Le Vasseur.) The crux of the matter for him is whether or not a man of principle is any better off than a man of pleasure—one of those insolvable problems that Boswell loved. That Boswell is never completely satisfied with any answers and continues his quest for more adds to the suspense that unifies these journals.

In a remarkable scene described by Boswell, he and Rousseau eat simply in Rousseau's kitchen and discuss another one of Boswell's intense interests: politics, specifically despotism vs. freedom in society. The scene is a remarkable one as a piece of travel literature because it is so intimate and so universal at the same time—the things Boswell does best. Boswell helps Thèrése Le Vasseur cook. He describes exactly what they eat: soup, vegetables, cold pork, stoned pears and chestnuts, and wine. It is a scene of domestic ease, yet as Boswell is certainly aware, he is sitting in the kitchen of the greatest writer in Europe asking him deep philosophical questions. The talk here moves naturally from table manners to politics. Boswell confesses that he, as laird of Auchinleck, is partial to despotism and that this worries him. This confession reminds him to ask Rousseau for a letter of introduction to General Paoli of the Corsicans. This opposition in Boswell of a love of monarchy, local despotism, and order vs. his real interest in the freedom movements such as that of General Paoli who led the Corsicans in their fight for freedom from Genoa is typical of Boswell's unsolvable conundrums.

Boswell takes these philosophical problems on to his other target, Voltaire. Perhaps because of the more lively and accessible social atmosphere of the Ferney household as compared to Rousseau's isolated retreat at Motiers, Boswell is less intimate with Voltaire and generally confines his questions to religion. In particular, Boswell defends traditional religion in the face of Voltaire's insistence on the lack of a soul. Clearly Boswell is just playing a role here, since his own views on religion are not at all set. Perhaps he senses that this is one issue in which he can engage the great thinker's attention and will be able to continue writing to him on the subject. The experience of trying out all these ideas on the two most famous thinkers in Europe is exhilarating for Boswell. After leaving Ferney, Boswell pauses in his journal to reflect upon the effect these visits have had upon him.

> What a singular being do I find myself! Let this my journal show what a variety my mind is capable of. But am I not well received everywhere? Am I not particularly taken notice of by men of the most distinguished genius? And why? I have neither profound knowl-

edge, strong judgement, nor constant gaiety. But I have a noble soul which still shines forth, a certain degree of knowledge, a multiplicity of ideas of all kinds, an original humour and turn of expression, and, I really believe, a remarkable knowledge of human nature. (*G&S*, 296)

It is just this dramatization of a processual self that is the central theme of Boswell's travel books.

As he crosses the Alps into Italy, Boswell must know that his days as a traveler are numbered. Prior to his departure from Britain, Boswell's father refused to provide funds for a tour of southern Europe. Now Boswell must constantly connive and cajole in order to be allowed to continue. One senses that what drives him on is his curiosity about himself more than the landscape, the people, or the cultural monuments that await him. One also senses that despite the intellectual discussions with Rousseau and Voltaire, Boswell is still not certain, in practice, who he is: libertine or husband; Deist or Anglican; despotic Scottish laird or champion of social freedom. In Italy, Boswell deliberately and totally gives way to his sensual desires, stalking married women and eventually having a serious affair with one. His preoccupation with sex is both offensive and comic. It is as though he has taken Rousseau's advice about being a citizen literally. His rationale is that sexual liberty is permissible in Italy because "the women are so debauched that they are hardly to be considered as moral agents, but as inferior beings" (*ICF*, 30). His sexual behavior, as always, generated religious conflict for Boswell and in his mind they are always linked.

In Rome he seems impressed by the Catholic mass. In his memorandum he notes the following: "Pope knelt and prayed. Whole crowd on knees. Universal silence, perfect devotion" (*ICF*, 65). Yet in a letter to his friend Temple, Boswell confesses to a more ecumenical view on the issue of religion. "In true philosophical frame I sat down and wrote a Tusculan Question on happiness, in which I considered religion. I was perfectly impartial, and calmly enquired how much more clear light has been imparted to the world during the eighteen hundred years that have rolled on since Cicero wrote his famous *Tusculan Questions*" (*ICF*, 68). In the essay he later writes on this subject, Boswell's position on religion is made clearer. As the editor of the *Grand Tour* reminds us, "In it [Boswell] accepts Christianity as one of the 'three or four great systems said to be sent from heaven' " (*ICF*, 68). Like the issue of sex, religious questions are not solved for Boswell on this tour of Italy, only made more complex.

What occupies Boswell after Italy serves neither sex nor religion. He turns his attention to the more tangible world of political freedoms. As we know from the meeting with Rousseau, Boswell had already taken a notion to see the freedom fighters of Corsica up close and had asked Rousseau for a letter of introduction. He is undoubtedly attracted to Corsica because of its reputation as an unspoiled Rousseauean feudal society, a land of noble savages struggling against a civilized and despotic European master. Their leader, General Pasquale de Paoli, is also reported to be of noble stature, brave, and well educated. Given Boswell's curiosity about both politics and people, it is not surprising that he would undertake a very dangerous and unusual journey to the heart of the Corsican resistance. Boswell makes his purpose clear at the beginning of the journal.

> I wished for something more than just the common course of what is called the tour of Europe; and Corsica occurred to me as a place which nobody else had seen, and where I should find what was to be seen nowhere else, a people actually fighting for liberty and forming themselves from a poor, inconsiderable, oppressed nation into a flourishing and independent state. (*ICF*, 156)

As travel writing, Boswell's description of this part of his tour is unsurpassed in focus, detail, and style. He keeps us attentive to the larger issue represented by Paoli and his band of fighters while at the same time giving us vignettes of people and places he meets, ending with a long portrait of the general himself. Stylistically, the Corsican journal is more like a traditional travel book. Boswell does not record his day by day activities, but employs more straightforward narration.

> In writing this Journal, I shall not tire my readers with relating the occurences of each particular day. It will be much more agreeable to them to have a free and continued account of what I saw or heard most worthy of observation. (*ICF*, 154)

This narrative decision has several effects. The compression of time, as Professor Brady points out (in a footnote to the passage above), makes it seem as if Boswell spends much more time with Paoli than he actually does. In addition, Boswell can become more of a traditional narrator while keeping himself in the background and reserving the foreground for the heroic Paoli. He also can heighten the tension and suspense this way, especially on the trip to the interior as he prepares to meet the fabled general. These techniques—the manipulation of time and space, the emphasis on narration vs. journal keeping—make the Corsican journal more like a modern travel book. Indeed it was published as a travel book when Boswell returned to England (*An Account of Corsica; The Journal of a Tour to That Island, and Memoirs of Pascal Paoli,* 1768), and it was very successful. The "Account of Corsica," added to the Corsican journal that Boswell kept during his journey, recounted historical and geographical information about the island, making the book a kind of two-part study of Corsica's land and its people, focusing on one of its bravest, General Paoli.

As narrator, Boswell adopts a peculiar stance, but one that serves his book well. Many times he describes himself as a "young traveler," and this is precisely the role he assumes—a rather young, impressionable, even hero-worshipping traveler. We have seen this role in the Grand Tour before but never as sustained. Here we sense that Boswell is either at the mercy of the Corsicans or at the feet of Paoli. Yet, as narrative stance, this works to force Boswell and all his self-consciousness into the background for once and let the people he meets occupy the foreground. Paradoxically, what we sense at work by the end of the Corsican journal is a bolder, more mature Boswell at work.

Boswell's attention to detail makes the trip to Corsica memorable. He describes the roads, the convents where he stays, and sometimes the mountains but always the people of Corsica. He adopts the ways of his guides, fetching chestnuts by the roadside; he describes in detail the methods of honey gathering by friars. He even holds conversations with prisoners in an effort to know everything about the Corsican nature. Only once does the Boswell of the Grand Tour surface, giving pompous, condescending advice to a group of Corsicans. All of this detail serves to focus the purpose of the trip on the eventual meeting with General Paoli. Corsicans with whom Boswell travels, eats, and sleeps all attest to the bravery and dignity of their leader. The obstacles along the way and the roughness of the trip all serve to move Boswell closer to his goal which is Paoli's camp in the mountainous interior of Corsica where no continental European had ever penetrated.

Upon his approach to Sollacaro, Boswell reveals a certain amount of anxiety and feelings of inferiority as the moment to meet Paoli draws near. The inferiority of narrative position is emphasized at this point. A small man is about to meet a large man, the narrative pacing slows considerably, and suddenly Boswell in is the presence of General Paoli. "I had stood in the presence of many a prince, but I never had such a trial as in the presence of Paoli" (*ICF*, 171).

Their first meeting between the wary General and the odd European before him, feverishly taking notes, is extremely tense. Once trust is established, however, Boswell can begin the work he has in mind: a detailed portrait of this general he has come so far to see.

The portrait is developed along the same lines that Boswell uses to unify the Grand Tour—his concerns with sex, politics, religion, and the nature of man in general. Now, however, we get only Paoli's views on the matters at hand, with Boswell keeping uncharacteristically quiet. During the week he is with Paoli, the two men talk much of politics and government, which are topics much in Paoli's mind. Democracy, social freedom, and patriotism are lauded by Paoli and, by reflection, Boswell. So too are the virtues of marriage and the exclusion of vice. Boswell's comments, although low key, are telling: "Were [Paoli] a libertine his influence would soon vanish, for men will never trust the importunate concern of society to one that they know will do what is hurtful to society for his own pleasures" (*ICF*, 177). He thinks it good advice to work toward "preserving young men from the contagion of vice" (*ICF*, 177). On religion Boswell agrees with Paoli on everything from God's existence to the working of divine providence in the affairs of the Corsicans. Nowhere do we see the argumentative, self-absorbed Boswell who is so intensely caught up in his own intellectual questions. At one point Boswell speaks of his melancholia, but the entry is so brief and so impersonal that the occasion is clearly to show Paoli's opinions on the subject.

Paoli has opinions on just about everything; he is evidently well read, thoughtful, and dedicated to his country. Everything the general says revolves around the fact of Paoli's dedication to the Corsican cause. This single-minded allegiance to Corsican independence focuses Paoli's passions, and it is probably this quality that appeals most to Boswell. It makes Paoli energetic, forceful, blunt—all the things Boswell wants to be himself. The cause gives Paoli answers that Boswell can never find; it gives Paoli a purpose for which Boswell yearns.

The argument that a post-Corsica Boswell is a more mature Boswell is only partly convincing. Indeed he seems to have more confidence socially, but his lack of confidence had never really held him back before. He doesn't seem to have resolved his libertine notions since he seduces Rousseau's mistress on the trip back to England. Upon his return, Boswell crusades for the Corsican cause in Britain, and while this political determination seems to be the work of a more mature, focused young man, Boswell is really only borrowing Paoli's purpose instead of finding one of his own. Where the Corsican journal does exhibit a mature Boswell is in its writer's biographic style. Only now is Boswell sure enough of his writing to be able to pull in close to a great figure and remain on the periphery. His silence enables him to observe all the quirks and nuances of behavior and record conversation in vivid detail. He is finally the Boswell mature enough in style to write the *Tour of the Hebrides* and the biography of Samuel Johnson.

There is no doubt that the tour as a whole has mellowed Boswell. "London has no longer that fascination which formerly blinded me" (*ICF*, 306). He has come full circle and clearly been changed by his three years abroad. Unlike most young men of his day, Boswell probably does profit from the Grand Tour, but only because Boswell himself wrings so much out of every moment and commits thoughts and deeds to paper while exposing his most intimate fantasies and follies. This kind of intense involvement is unique to travel writing in Boswell's time but would soon set a new standard for the writers to come.

# Chapter 3

## VICTORIAN WOMEN TRAVELERS: MARY KINGSLEY

Although some women traveled abroad in the eighteenth century, notably Lady Mary Wortley Montagu, it is not really until the nineteenth century that women begin to travel alone to distant places far from the confines of home. Gertrude Bell, a traveler herself, speaks passionately for this group of women travelers.

> To those bred under an elaborate social order few such moments of exhilaration can come as that which stands at the threshold of wild travel. The gates of the enclosed garden are thrown open, the chain at the entrance of the sanctuary is lowered, with a wary glance to right and left you step forward, and, behold! the immeasurable world.[1]

The generation of women for whom Bell speaks was born in the mid–nineteenth century into a world that typically restricted women's movements away from the home. Indeed, for centuries, travel for women meant traveling with a male chaperone, often in ι group of women or, more likely, with one's husband. To travel alone, even as late as the mid–nineteenth century, was considered a dangerous and probably licentious endeavor for a woman to undertake. The ecstatic release that Gertrude Bell invokes in her opening passage to *Syria: The Desert and the Sown* (1907) was a relatively rare experience for women who were products of that "elaborate social order" of Victorian England.[2]

The increased democratization of travel and, perhaps more important, the gradual democratization of a woman's role in society during the nineteenth century allowed a significant number of well-educated, upper-class single women to journey to remote places. Their names are legendary: Isabella Bird riding her Arabian horse through the mountain passes of Central Asia; Isabella Eberhardt, disguised as an Arab boy, wandering North Africa in search of eroticism and danger; Marianne North traveling and painting on five continents; and Mary Kingsley in pursuit of fish and fetish in West Africa's interior. Their stories are surprisingly similar. Raised as "the scholarly one," not destined for marriage or married off unhappily, many of these women spent their youths dutifully caring for husbands or ailing parents. But when "the gates of the enclosed garden are thrown open" a desire for "wild travel" commands the rest of their lives.

Victorian women, perhaps still feeling that duty to "home," often required a scientific or artistic mission to frame their travels. Isabella Bird's books are full of what amount to sociological discourses on traditional crafts and customs of Persia, or economic analyses of Arab trade and labor in the region. Mary Kingsley devotes hundreds of pages to the religious fetish systems of West Africans. Marianne North traveled as a botanical artist and exhibited her paintings at the Royal Botanical Gardens. Yet anyone who reads these books is struck by the sense of awe and curiosity with which these women travel. Despite the avowed scientific purpose of the trip, it is the "immeasurable world" that really keeps them going.

Despite their rigorous endeavors and the new information they often brought back, their public reception was mixed. Learned groups, eager to hear tales from abroad, asked Kingsley, Bird, North, and others to speak at their meetings. Yet their reputation rested more on their speaking ability than their travels, so that formal respect and inclusion in the all-male world of travel was slow to come. Indeed, after a lengthy battle with the Royal Geographic

Society, a handful of women travelers were eventually asked to become fellows in 1913. The popular press was especially unkind. Cartoons of the day show Kingsley or Bird perched precariously on camel or canoe, sandwiched in between groups of natives, looking ridiculously out of place in their dresses and bonnets. This kind of treatment trivialized their efforts and was largely responsible for them being seen as freaks. Kinder critics praised them as examples of the "new women" and lumped all women travelers and suffragettes together. This more positive marginalizing of their role as women infuriated travelers like Mary Kingsley even more than the satiric cartoons because Kingsley, Bell, and others were adamantly opposed to the women's suffrage movement.[3]

This perhaps ironic need to both establish independence from the prevailing norms for women and at the same time reaffirm one's traditional femininity is an interesting starting place for an examination of the contribution of women travelers of the nineteenth century to the genre of travel literature. The question of their dress exemplifies this dichotomy. Even the most rigorous travelers like Mary Kingsley and Isabella Bird, obliged to camp in native houses or to hunt specimens in dangerous rapids, insisted on proper female dress: long skirts, blouses, and stout stays. For Kingsley, at least, the insistence on difference was a matter of asserting one's established role and not presuming to overstep one's bounds as a woman. This leads her to a revealing speculation about the place of women. In her appendix to *Travels in West Africa* she argues against prevailing missionary opinion that the difference between European and African people is one of degree—that the African is a lesser human being.

> The bad effects that have arisen from [missionary] teaching have come primarily from the failure of the missionary to recognize the difference between the African and themselves as being a difference not of degree but of kind. . . . I feel certain that a black man is no more an undeveloped white man than a rabbit is an undeveloped hare; and the mental difference between the two races is very similar to that between men and women among ourselves.[4]

When Kingsley aligns men with Europe and women with the colonized other, a curious thing happens. We are invited to see the woman traveler as a different kind of traveler, one whose ways of seeing and assessing people and places outside Europe might just be different in kind as well. Let us look closely at Mary Kingsley herself and her great work on West Africa as a way of accepting that invitation.

The few critics who have analyzed the literary contribution of women travelers tend to agree that there is a curious tension in the writing of nineteenth-century women. Sara Mills's work on women's travel writing and colonialism is a fine example of the appreciation of this kind of tension.[5] Her book argues that there is a complex relationship between the narratives of some women writers and the prevailing male society in whose name much of the world is colonized. Mills discovers in Mary Kingsley's work, for example, that although her text aligns itself with colonial practices and traditional feminine values, there is also a constant subversion of these two positions. Although Mills is content to allow the open position to stand as an invitation to read these texts within the context of colonial discourse, Dea Birkett's study of Victorian women travelers, *Spinsters Abroad* (1989), tends to isolate the texts and tries to account for this paradoxical viewpoint of the nineteenth-century woman travel writer.[6] She sees the woman's emotional response to the world, particularly the sympathy with politically subjugated people, as an anticolonialist response driven in part by the sense of identification with those who are outside the patriarchal power structures both at home and abroad. Birkett's assumption that these women disapproved of colonialist intervention stems from her observation that travelers such as Kingsley and Bell consistently glorified the precolonial native society—the world of the "pure Arab" or the "unadulterated African." She assumes that this yearning for a primitive utopia derives from the travelers' sense of themselves as colonialized women living in a patriarchal Victorian society (Birkett, 164).

As we have just seen in the Mary Kingsley passage, however, the racial assumptions about difference were still evident and, for Kingsley at least, a rationale for imperialism. For although she argues vehemently against some colonial practices, she still advocates imperialist motivation for the occupation of West Africa. Birkett acknowledges the woman's viewpoint this way.

When woman travellers emphasized essential differences between people they were both supporting racial assumptions which claimed the Savage or the Oriental could never be a European, and, at the same time, challenging them through their . . . appeal to judge the exotic societies on their terms. (Birkett, 165)

In a curious way, then, for these women to emphasize difference was to defend the native culture. And, to be sure, nineteenth-century women travelers tend to stand firmly on the side of cultural relativism while paradoxically defending the need for a European guiding hand.

Another study of nineteenth century women writers, *Madwoman in the Attic* (1979), offers an intriguing thesis that helps to explain the often inconsistent themes of the Victorian women who told stories.[7] Sandra Gilbert and Susan Gubar argue that, although trapped by "patriarchal poetry," nineteenth century women novelists found a subversive way to voice their own feminine concerns. Like their sister writers, women travelers were trapped not by "patriarchal poetry," but by patriarchal politics which demanded that England bring order to the world and that the sun never set on the British Empire. And like the women novelists who found a way to "write back" using traditional male forms, women travel writers may have found a way to subvert the message of racism and colonialism through a kind of cultural relativism and honest sympathy with native people.

This kind of subversion would also explain the dual message of scientific research and a love of "wild travel" for its own sake that we see in so many Victorian women travelers, especially Mary Kingsley. It may also explain the haunting pattern of imagery in Kingsley's prose that moves from imprisonment to escape. And finally, for Kingsley, this double voice may occur in the very style of her writing which says, "I am a sane witty, proper English woman, afraid of nothing" but whose very actions fly in the face of that description. To borrow a phrase from Emily Dickinson, Mary Kingsley "dances like a bomb abroad" (quoted in Gilbert and Gubar, 85). Like the women studied in *Madwoman in the Attic*, Mary Kingsley and her counterparts express themselves through "mad doubles" who voice "their claustrophobic rage by enacting rebellious escape" (Gilbert and Gubar, 85). The women travelers, however, are able to do this literally and then find a way of expressing that mad experience of "escaping into the open spaces of their own authority" through their writing (Gilbert and Gubar, 83).

Mary Kingsley's abrupt departure for West Africa amounts to nothing less than an escape. As a shy child of middle class parents, Kingsley lived most of her childhood and early adulthood within the confines of the house and garden at Highgate in England. Her father was an eccentric doctor who preferred travel and ethnology to medical practice. During the long months and years he was away, the young Kingsley spent most of her time in his library reading, educating herself with his eclectic collection of books. She lived for his return when the house would be filled with his travel stories. As her parents aged, the household duties fell upon the daughter who literally cared for both parents until they died within six weeks of each other in 1892. At 30 years of age, with no experience and no specific training, she found herself free for the first time, "feeling," as she says, "like a boy with a new half crown" (*Africa*, 1). That this woman would choose to exercise that freedom by traveling alone to such a dangerous and unmapped terrain is remarkable. But by the next year she was in West Africa. In all she made two trips. Her 700-page book, *Travels in West Africa*, is about the second adventure and is a testament not only to her bravery and stamina, but also to her uncanny ability to remain the dutiful, proper middle-aged spinster from Highgate.

This kind of paradoxical doubling occurs throughout her work. Even her avowed scientific purpose for going abroad stands in sharp contrast with her lyric passages of the beauty of West Africa. Trained by her father to catalogue his specimens for his collection, Mary Kingsley preferred to tell people that she was going to West Africa to continue her father's work. As a "daughter of the patriarchy" this impulse had the advantage of being useful, and complemented her role as dutiful daughter. She sums up the purpose for both journeys with the phrase "in pursuit of fish and fetish." The fish were destined for the British Museum and her interest in religions of the region she owed to her father's passion for ethnology. Indeed, much of the later half of the book is devoted to these findings. Several long chapters deal exclusively with the religions and spiritual practices of the various peoples she encounters, and she includes a vast appendix that catalogues the fish and insects she has brought back in her collecting jars. But the book is about so much more. There is throughout a kind of double theme not unlike the duty/desire paradox of Boswell: on one hand we see Mary Kingsley dutifully collecting fish for the museum, while at the same time deliberately taking risks and having adventures for their own sake. If scientific duty for fish and fetish bring her to West Africa, it is the desire to experience the wild beauty of the place that keeps her there.

*Travels in West Africa* is less about collecting than it is about seeing. Kingsley spends an inordinate amount of prose describing the intricacies of river, forest, and mountain. Her love of "wild travel" makes these passages come alive as no scientific journal could. The rivers of West Africa are her favorite places and she spends much time describing their habits.

> There is a uniformity in the habits of the West Coast rivers, from the Volta to the Coanza, which is, when you get used to it, very taking. Excepting the Congo, the really great river comes out to sea with as much mystery as possible; lounging lazily along among its mangrove swamps in a what's-it-matter-when-one-comes-out and where's-the-hurry style, through quantities of channels inter-communicating with each other. (*Africa*, 87)

It is while on these mysterious rivers that Kingsley feels most alive.

> Indeed, much as I have enjoyed life in Africa, I do not think I ever enjoyed it to the full as I did on those nights dropping down the Rembwé. The great, black, winding river with a pathway in its midst of frosted silver where the moonlight struck it: on either side the ink black mangrove walls, and above them the band of star and moonlit heavens that the walls of mangrove allowed one to see. Forward rose the form of our sail, idealized from bedsheetdom to glory; and the little red glow of our cooking fire gave a single note of warm colour to the cold light of the moon. (*Africa*, 338)

No ordinary Victorian naturalist, Kingsley clearly places herself at great risk learning to navigate the rivers, the forests, and the mountains. She is a traveler bent on learning the lessons this region has to offer and experiencing its dangers as well as its beauties. She writes at length about learning how to "see" in the forest.

> On first entering the great grim twilight regions of the forest you hardly see anything but the vast column-like grey tree stems in the

countless thousands around you, and the sparsely vegetated ground beneath. But day by day, as you get trained to your surroundings, you see more and more and a whole world grows up gradually out of the gloom before your eyes. (*Africa*, 101)

The sense one gets is that this woman is literally waking up and seeing a whole new world for the first time. Undoubtedly this kind of attention to detail makes her a better naturalist, but it is the wildness and beauty of the African landscape that speaks to her heart. Under the guise of scientific duty, Mary Kingsley can express the awe and reverence she has for raw nature, where "once you know it . . . you bow down and worship" (*Africa*, 550).

This new way of knowing and the heightened feelings she experiences on the river and in the forest are directly linked to images of escape. Not being able to see in this new way is likened by Kingsley to "being shut up in a library whose books you cannot read, all the while tormented, terrified, and bored" (*Africa*, 102). One hears in this phrase a lifetime of confinement and cloistered existence where knowledge and escape are directly linked to reading. In the forest and on the rivers, seeing becomes a way for her to literally escape her former existence. She explains this more explicitly during a dangerous trip down the rapids of the Ogowé.

> The majesty and beauty of the scene fascinated me, and I stood leaning with my back against a rock pinnacle watching it. Do not imagine it gave rise, in what I am pleased to call my mind, to those complicated, poetical reflections natural beauty seems to bring out in other people's minds. It never works that way with me; I just lose all sense of human individuality, all memory of human life, with its grief and worry and doubt, and become part of the atmosphere. (*Africa*, 178)

This is a remarkably revealing passage about the ultimate escape from self that we sense is at the bottom of her love of West Africa. The contrast with her former life is palpable; for her the "majesty and beauty" of nature offer an escape from self, duty, even her own scientific objectives.

Another kind of escape that she experiences is the release from the submissive, duty-bound female role of her former life to that of power and authority as sole leader of her small expeditions. But, as we have seen, this escape is paradoxically bound by her insistence on remaining—in outer form at least—determinedly female. Perhaps it is significant that she identifies with a small "boy" with a new half crown as she contemplates her newfound freedom. For it is with assured power and authority that she directs her ragtag group of natives through rapids and up mountains. Indeed they call her "Sir," follow her directions (usually unwillingly), and defer to her judgement in times of confusion or conflict.

Another way this duality between authority and submissiveness is played out is in her writing style. There is a curious dichotomy between how she tells about her travels and what she actually does. Early in her book we see a tendency to assume the narrative stance of a proper Victorian lady, while telling stories no such lady ought to know.

> But I must forthwith stop writing about the Gold Coast, or I shall go on telling you stories and wasting your time not to mention the danger of letting out those which would damage the nerves of the cultured and temperate climes, such as those . . . of the man who wore brass buttons; the moving story of three leeches and two gentlemen; the doctor up a creek; and the reason why you should not eat pork along here because all the natives have either got the guinea-worm, or kraw-kraw or ulcers; and then the pigs go and—dear me! it was a near thing that time. I'll leave off at once. (*Africa*, 41)

This prim hesitancy to discuss matters of personal hygiene (and whatever else was implied in these sketches) extends to her own adventures as well. Kingsley's prim, ladylike prose insists that, as one critic has put it, "to hack away through the densest rainforests of the Congo, to be fired at by hostile savages or charged by wild beasts, was scarcely more than a stroll through Hyde Park on a wet afternoon."[8] Often Kingsley resorts to telling her stories of danger in the second person, as if to distance herself even more from the grisly proceedings. On one occasion she is trapped in a mangrove swamp at low tide and must wait, amid crocodiles, for the tide to release her canoe.

> [I]f you are a mere ordinary person of a retiring nature like me, you stop in your lagoon until the tide rises again; most of your attention is directed to dealing with an "at home" to crocodiles and mangrove flies, and with the fearful stench of the slime round you. . . . Twice

this chatty little incident, as Lady MacDonald would call it, happened to me. (*Africa*, 89)

The "chatty little incident" continues with an amazing story of a crocodile clambering into her canoe, "endeavoring to improve [her] acquaintance." She dispatches it with a swift blow to the snout with her paddle and admonishes the creature for not having "learnt manners." This kind of witty, ironic prose that depends on British allusions to manner and society is the chief source of Kingsley's brand of humor. As in all irony, this kind of humor emphasizes the gap between expectation and reality. In this way Kingsley can further emphasize her retiring, ladylike position as Victorian woman, and at the same time be the voice of adventure, escape, and authority.

On one of the occasions when she is "charged by wild beasts," her way of telling the tale both emphasizes her role as prim lady in the bush, and at the same time reveals what usually passes for masculine adroitness and bravery.

> I have never hurt a leopard intentionally; I am habitually kind to animals, and besides I do not think it is ladylike to go shooting things with a gun. (*Africa*, 545)

Nonetheless she breaks up a fight between a leopard and a native dog and then fends off the leopard, who is about to charge her, with a well-aimed toss of a water jar.

> The leopard crouched, I think to spring on me. I can see its great, beautiful, lambent eyes still, and I seized an earthen water-cooler and flung it straight at them. It was a noble shot; it burst upon the leopard's head like shell. (*Africa*, 46)

Her arch self-effacement continues in this manner when asked by the people in the village twenty minutes later if anything was the matter. "I civilly asked them to go and ask the leopard in the bush" (*Africa*, 546). This passage is remarkable in other ways as well because it reveals, as do so many other passages, Kingsley's recognition of the wild beauty in Africa, even (or perhaps particularly) in a moment of heightened danger.

This duality of style and content—the ironic, self-effacing prose that renders even dangers like these as cooly comic adventures—

ultimately becomes rather tedious. One longs for the intense passages on the river or in the dimly lit jungle where she does not distance herself so much from her adventures. But *Travels in West Africa* is a book of many voices, and one of those voices is Mary Kingsley, daughter of Dr. George Henry Kingsley, dutifully bound to the society that raised her to be a woman of class and manners. Another voice is that of a remarkably strong and fierce woman who is apparently afraid of nothing and who loves the dangers and wilds of Africa more than she does the confines of Highgate.

These same two voices also compete in the political arena as Kingsley, on one hand, champions England's right and duty to gain more territory in West Africa and, on the other, argues for a kind of cultural relativism not usually associated with imperialism. In the social and political sections of her book, she argues that "civilization" of Africa by Europe has not helped the people of that continent.

> Nothing strikes one so much, in studying the degeneration of these native tribes, as the direct effect that civilization and reformation has in hastening it. The worst enemy to the existence of the African tribe, is the one who comes to it and says:—Now you must civilize, and come to school, and leave off all those awful goings-on of yours, and settle down quietly. (*Africa*, 403)

Much of her anger at these practices is leveled at the European missionary who, she argues, does not honor the native religious and social practices but insists that the native tribes give up completely what they have always known. However, Kingsley keenly observes what contemporary anthropological observers are saying today: a subjugated people do not totally abandon their own culture but, instead, take what they want from the dominant culture and keep what they like of their own after first removing "all the disagreeable parts" (*Africa*, 403).[9] For Kingsley this practice is "a very bad thing for [the African]" (*Africa*, 403) because he has no foothold in either his or the dominant culture and is caught between the demands of both. Kingsley is unusually sympathetic to native practices and challenges the prevailing popular assumptions about the savagery of the African.

> Indeed, when one lives out here and sees the surrounding conditions of this state of culture, the conviction grows on you that, morally

speaking, the African is far from being the brutal fiend he is often painted. . . . The African [is] not; and through his culture does not contain our institutions, lunatic asylums, prisons, workhouses, hospitals, &c., he has to deal with the same class of people who require these things. So with them he deals by means of his equivalent institutions, slavery, the lash, and death. (*Africa*, 499)

In passages like these that deal with the social and religious customs of the tribes she visits, Kingsley argues for an understanding of these customs through the eyes and hearts of the African, instead of the customary European view.

Kingsley is not, however, free of Eurocentrism and racism. As we have seen, she believes difference in race to be one of kind; as rabbits and hares are different, so are men and women, and so are Europeans and Africans. Despite her naturally intellectually and sympathetically based belief in a kind of cultural relativism, Kingsley firmly believes that the African is in need of the European to relieve his or her mind of its "pretty muddle" (*Africa*, 501). Instead of church and school, however, Kingsley would prefer technical training with more emphasis on economics than religion. Her natural sympathies are with the precolonial native, perhaps, as Dea Birkett suggests, because as a woman she understands the nature of subjugation by a patriarchal society of rule makers. As close as she ever comes to being anticolonial occurs near the end of Appendix One on "Trade and Labour in West Africa" where she advises the British government to understand the nature of her beloved trader and to give him more territory and more support. Yet she cannot help but reveal her true sympathies.

> There is a certain school of philanthropists in Europe who say that it is not advisable to spread white trade in Africa, that the native is provided by the Bountiful Earth with all that he really requires, and that therefore he should be allowed to live his simple life, and not be compelled or urged to work for the white man's gain. I have a sneaking sympathy with these good people, because I like the African in his bush-state best. (*Africa*, 677)

She goes on to argue for the reverse of this sentiment as a prowhite trader because, as she says, the bountiful earth does not provide much to these Africans but a poor hand-to-mouth existence. In the end, even her colonialist stance derives from her sympathy with the native. She ends Appendix One with this final statement on the subject.

> I do not believe that the white race will ever drag the black up to their own particular summit in the mountain range of civilization. Both polygamy and slavery are, for divers reasons, essential to the well-being of Africa—at any rate for those vast regions of it which are agricultural, and these two institutions will necessitate the African having a summit to himself. Only—alas! for the energetic reformer—the African is not keen on mountaineering in the civilization range. He prefers remaining down below and being comfortable. He is not conceited about this; he admires the higher culture very much, and the people who inconvenience themselves by going in for it—but do it himself? NO. And if he is dragged up into the higher regions of a self-abnegatory religion, six times in ten he falls back damaged, a morally maimed man, into his old swampy country fashion valley. (*Africa*, 680)

What is most interesting about this passage is that Mary Kingsley applies these very same standards of autonomy and self-awareness to herself. As she insists that the Africans be left to their own cultural practices which are "essential to the well-being of Africa" and which will provide the basis for a "summit to himself," Kingsley also insists that, as a woman of her own culture and society, she maintain those standards with which she was raised—dress, manners, devotion to duty, and sympathy with those less fortunate than herself. She wants her own "summit," not that of a man or of a "new woman." Both the style and the content of *Travels in West Africa* depend on this self-imposed standard of authenticity. Her humor particularly depends on it. But this gender-based irony would not be available much longer to women travelers. As more and more women traveled, this source of coy humor would seem antiquated and even ridiculous. For Kingsley it works because much of what she says about West Africa depends upon a double or even triple vision. The caring, proper Victorian spinster who dutifully collects rare fish can also sympathetically collect religious myths and practices without labeling their source as savage. This properly dressed woman, who blanches at the thought of the impropriety of a lost stay in her blouse, also has the same self-assurance to fend off crocodiles and leopards. The different voices of Mary Kingsley are a product of her society and her world; the essential strength of character that unifies these voices is her own.

Women's voices continue to tell stories about foreign places, despite the fact that their texts have been far less well received than those of their male counterparts. One reason for this is that the genesis of women's authorship was typically found in the private sphere: in diaries, letters, and photo albums—texts that remained close to the home and family. Paradoxically perhaps, travel writing's close connection to these kinds of texts, especially the memoir, allowed women entry into the travel genre, even though respect for their books would be delayed. As we have seen, Egeria's text about the Holy Land is in the form of a letter, as are Lady Mary Wortley Montagu's impressions of Turkey. It is not until the late nineteenth century that women begin to regularly produce the more "factual" (and less confessional) travel books that men were publishing. Mary Kingsley's book is a good example of this new trend. Yet, even after women move into the sphere of book publishing and produce travel texts on a par with men, their efforts are still marginalized. As Sarah Mills reminds us, "there is a tradition of reading women's writing as trivial or as marginal to the mainstream, and this is certainly the attitude to women's travel writing" (Mills, 61). Mills argues that women's travel writing has had to negotiate many literary conventions and social discourses that ultimately determine both how the books are produced and how they are received by the public. In particular these are the generic conventions of travel writing and, for nineteenth-century women, colonial discourses. Mills finds, as I do in this chapter on Kingsley, that many of the conventions of travel writing—the monarch-of-all-I-survey position, the male domination of a female-gendered landscape, or the traditionally male narrator-adventurer role—may or may not be used by women, and that the other, more subversive voices used to resist these conventions are not lesser voices because they are not male, but ought to be considered and read as complex, new contributions to the genre.

For women traveling and writing today much has changed. The discourse of feminism, for instance, can now influence the texts of women travel writers in ways unavailable to Gertrude Bell or Mary Kingsley. The general acceptance in the late twentieth century of women as more equal to men means that their travels to difficult places, their roles as leaders and adventurers are more readily accepted by a contemporary reading and publishing public more willing to read women writers on their own terms. However, it is clear that women's travel writing is still considered somewhat of an anomaly. In the three influential *Granta* issues on travel (1984, 1986, 1989) that launched many new travel writers such as Bruce Chatwin, Ryszard Kapuściński, and Jonathan Raban, only two women—Martha Gellhorn and Jan Morris—are included among the twenty or so male writers. Likewise, in this study by a woman, only one woman is awarded a full chapter. There must be, as Sarah Mills argued for Victorian women, still some constraints on both the production and reception of women's travel writing. Even today, men simply travel more and get their books published more readily than women do. This is true, however, not only of women, but also of the majority of the world that is not white, Western, upper middle class, and educated. To travel with the express purpose of writing books is a privileged activity not available to large portions of the world's population. It should come as no surprise, then, that the world of travel writers is a small one, and is a world only recently assailed by women.

A 1993 book, *Maiden Voyages*, which seeks to correct the omissions of women from other anthologies, does focus on a wide array of women figures in travel writing but, while doing an admirable job of focusing the spotlight on women, also undermines any future reconciliation of men and women as travel writers by reasserting the idea that women travel writers are special. The book's editor, Mary Morris, a travel writer herself, insists on the essential difference beween women's texts and men's; she cites women's concern with the internal journey, for instance, as one of the chief differences. This kind of critical stance is ultimately dangerous, since it still serves to marginalize women as writers of the confessional mode, rather than allowing us to see them as part of the conversation that is travel writing, a discourse that includes the confessional and the autobiographical. Morris's anthology is nonetheless valuable because it introduces remarkable writers whose travel books should never be overlooked: Flora Tristan, Mary Wollstonecraft, Isabella Bird, Anna Leonowens, Gertrude Bell, Kate Marsden, Edith Wharton, Willa Cather, Isak Dinesen, Rebecca West, Beryl Markham, Dervla Murphy, Joan Didion, and Annie Dillard.

Chapter 4

---

# THE MODERN PSYCHOLOGICAL JOURNEY: GRAHAM GREENE

During the period in European history known familiarly as "between the wars," the modern travel book as a literary genre became firmly established. Not only because, as we have seen in chapter 1, so many accomplished writers were producing excellent travel books, but also because these travel books from the 1920s and 1930s found a way to create metaphors about a shattered, anxious European world. As Paul Fussell argues, the modern period, with its dominant mood of discontent and self-examination, was peculiarly suited not only to exiles living and writing abroad, but also to books that offered travel as metaphor. Perhaps this is because the travel metaphor, what Samuel Hynes has called "the basic trope of the generation" (Hynes, 229), so ably served poetry and the novel during this period. In particular, the theme of self-discovery or, more accurately, the search for a shattered and scattered self that one sees in much modernist literature is itself often expressed in terms of travel. Eliot's "Little Gidding" is but one example.

We shall not cease from exploration
And the end of all our exploring
Will be to arrive where we started
And know the place for the first time.[1]

We also know from the structure and themes of *Ulysses*, *The Waste Land*, *The Sun Also Rises*, *A Passage to India*, *Goodbye to Berlin*, and *Journey's End* that whatever "modern" is, travel and anxiety are central to it.

Graham Greene's travel books are perhaps the best example of what Hynes calls "a dual plane work with a strong realistic surface, which is yet a parable" (Hynes, 228). Greene's first travel book, *Journey without Maps* (1936), chronicles an exhausting four-week trek deep into the uncharted Liberian forest. This "plane" is fairly typical of most travel books of his time, following the man-against-nature pattern. For Greene, however, this trip provides an opportunity for another, more personal journey in which the journey itself is transformed into a metaphor for psychological introspection. It is this other plane that marks Greene's travel books as the real beginning of heightened subjectivity in the genre. On perhaps even another level, Greene's personal sources of madness mirror the peculiar modern temperament of Europe between the wars. The images of modern man as alone, fearful, and alienated correspond to Greene the traveler. While Waugh's travel books comment on the social and political folly of all human beings, Greene's travel books reflect the personal anxiety of a fearful, haunted man, running blindly for cover in a world without faith. Greene's books are always about something else. They are clearly dual, perhaps even triple-layered, and as much about their author and the places he visits as they are about the ideas central to the 1920s and 1930s.

Travel has always provided Greene with a trope for understanding the search for meaning, both personal and philosophical. In "Lost Childhood," a 1947 essay written about his childhood, Greene outlines some of the themes that would occupy him for a lifetime of writing. In this essay Greene pays homage to the adventure/travel books he read as a child. They seem to have affected him on two levels. He admits that these books about faraway, exotic places are undoubtedly responsible for his need to travel and work in foreign places. But he also claims that books like Marjorie Bowen's *The Viper of Milan*, a story of war and intrigue between rival factions in sixteenth-century Italy, led him to be a writer. To the 14-year-old Greene, her book made writing seem possible, and it would give him his greatest theme: "perfect evil walking the world where perfect good can never walk again."[2] What is most interesting, however, in these ruminations of a 43-year-old man about his childhood is the language he uses to describe that formative period in his life. "One had lived for fourteen years in a wild jungle country without a map" (*Essays*, 17). Ten years after his first trip to West Africa, the sense of being mapless in a jungle stays with Greene as a haunting evocation of a "lost childhood," the time before books would show him the way out.

This predilection of Greene's, to conflate journey with childhood, is strongest in his first travel book, *Journey without Maps* (1936). In a very revealing introduction written in 1978 but absent from the 1980 Penguin edition, Greene discusses, among other things, travel writing in the 1930s, his cousin's role in the journey, and his decision to "make memory the very subject of this book."[3] Acknowledging the other popular writers of his time, Peter Fleming and Evelyn Waugh, Greene says (clearly speaking for himself), "We were a generation brought up on adventure stories who had missed the enormous disillusionment of the First War; so we went looking for adventure" (*Maps*, ix). But of his own efforts to write an "adventure" book about Liberia, Green had serious doubts. His notes, "written in pencil with increasing fatigue" (*Maps*, xi), his scraps of momentos and photographs do not seem, upon his return to England, enough to constitute a travel book. But it is his memories that he most doubts: "memories chiefly of rats, of frustration, and of a deeper boredom on the long forest trek than I had ever experienced before. How was I, out of all this, to make a book?" (*Maps*, xi). Lack of models was not the source of Greene's problem. Peter Fleming's books about his exotic adventures in China and Siberia with and without the rugged Ella Maillart made for popular reading because they were so much like youthful adventure stories. Evelyn Waugh's travel books with their surgical wit, passing judgment on politics and society wherever their author traveled, were also published by the time Greene began writing about his Liberian journey. Yet neither model would serve Greene's intentions in the end.

I was haunted by the awful tedium of A to Z. This book could not be written in the manner of a European tour; ... nor was it a political book in the sense that Gide's *Voyage au Congo* was political, nor a book of adventure like those of Mr. Peter Fleming—if this was an adventure it was only a subjective adventure. (*Maps*, xii)

This struggle with form and with the available models from the genre forces Greene to write a new kind of travel book, a psychological travel book about the journey inward as well as outward. "The account of a journey—a slow foot-sore journey into an interior literally unknown—was only of interest if it paralleled another journey" (*Maps*, xii). That journey would take Greene back, via memory, into the mapless jungle of his childhood and adolescence.

This need to rationalize the journey as a way of looking at the mapless self is reflected in the epigraphs Greene chooses for his first travel book.

"O do you imagine," said fearer to farer,
"That dusk will delay on your path to the pass,
Your diligent looking discover the lacking
Your footsteps feel from granite to grass?"

In this stanza by Auden, Greene is clearly interested in the themes of travel and of fear. These two sides of Greene himself are at constant odds in *Journey without Maps*. He is at times the fearer, wondering why he went at all. At other times he is the farer, sure that the journey has a point, a goal, a boon. The second epigraph, by Oliver Wendell Holmes, explains further why, despite the fears and the stupidity of dangerous travel, Greene sees the trip as a necessary psychological undertaking.

The life of an individual is in many respects like a child's dissected map. If I could live a hundred years ... I feel as if I could put the pieces together until they made a properly connected whole.

Here the theme of the individual's fragmented psyche is described in terms of a map, much as Greene describes himself in "Lost Childhood," so that the motifs of the journey, being lost, and a desire for wholeness prefigure these same themes in *Journey without Maps*.

The subject of maps dominates this book. There are three kinds of maps, all acting as metaphors for each other. The kinds of maps Holmes and Greene, in his childhood essay, are describing are personal, psychological maps, those byways into our past that connect us to our present which, when followed, presumably lead us to a place called Who We Are. The literal geographical maps of Liberia that Greene finds so confounding parallel these psychological maps because they are so misleading and so mysterious. Before setting out for West Africa, Greene tries to obtain some maps of the area but finds several versions, all equally unhelpful. The British General Staff's version of Liberia "quite openly confesses their ignorance" (*Maps*, 45). Liberia's interior is a large white space, empty except for a few arbitrary rivers and place names that bear no resemblance to native ones. Another map, issued by the U.S. War Department has, as Greene says, "a dashing quality about it" (*Maps*, 46). Where the British map has a blank space, the American version fills the space with the word "Cannibals." This American map, suggesting unknown roads in dotted lines in its unwillingness to confess its ignorance, is even dangerous despite its imaginatively labeled areas of "Dense Forest" and "Cannibals." The complete arbitrariness and outright falsity of competing versions of a geographic area should suggest to Greene that psychological maps are also subject to arbitrary constructs, that when we think we understand the mapless soul, we are merely constructing a map according to our own prejudices and desires. And, in a way, this is exactly what Greene does in *Journey without Maps*, minus the self-reflexivity. The whole or map he finally makes out of Liberia, the book itself, is a product of Greene's own fears and desires, a peculiar, haunted Liberia, that may or may not bear any resemblance to the place itself.

This brings us to the third kind of map—a cultural one. What Greene tries but does not succeed very well at is to navigate different cultural waters. He lacks any cultural maps, any sense of the culture of the places he visits, aside from the master-slave conditioning he receives from various British officials before leaving home. But to his credit Greene is sensitive to his lack of these types of signposts. Over and over he chastises himself for hurrying, for not taking the time to learn the secrets of the primitive, yet he hurries on, marching 8 to 10 hours a day, arriving exhausted and undramatically at the coast. Whatever he learns about himself or the Liberian people was learned during the writing of the book, not during the journey itself. The motif of mapping, then, occurs to Greene as he is planning the book. It is a way of writing a travel book "about something else," and it is Greene's greatest contribution to the genre,

As Greene tells us in the 1978 introduction, *Journey without Maps* is specifically about memory. For Greene, Africa is a piece of the dissected child's map that, when returned to its original position, can connect him to a specific sense of childhood fear, where terror is nameless and, more often than not, intimately bound to pleasure. Early in the book Greene makes this connection very clear. In a chapter that stands between his leaving England and his arriving in Sierra Leone, Greene explores the idea that Africa for him is "like a reminder of darkness" (*Maps*, 35). It is here that we begin to understand the complexity of Greene's own personal maps and the way in which he will use memory as a subtext for this travel book. After describing the boat's passengers in fairly typical travel genre style—seedy expatriates, exotic Moham-medans—Greene focuses on the Captain's killing of a hawk.

> The Captain took his gun and shot a hawk which sat in the rigging, the gulls scattered, twisting in the glittering air, and the dusty body plunged through them on to the deck, like a reminder of darkness. (*Maps*, 35)

The beauty of the gulls and the "glittering air" is commingled with the death and dusty body of the hawk, and it is this theme of pain and pleasure that Greene explores through memory in the chapter that follows, called "The Shape of Africa." The chapter begins with a repetition of the words, "a reminder of dark-ness" and then presents a series of personal memories in which happiness is intertwined with pain: a woman weeping in a bar in Leicester Square, ("You don't weep unless you've been happy first"); a flight into Berlin at night ("that was happiness"), mixed with an acute awareness of the swastikas and the pain on the ground; and finally, going far back to his childhood, the memory of a dead dog being placed in his pram with him by his nurse. Greene finally returns to the memory of the weeping girl that begins this section and says,

I thought for some reason even then of Africa, not a particular place, but a shape, a strangeness, a wanting to know. The unconscious mind is often sentimental; I have written "a shape," and the shape, of course, is roughly that of the human heart. (*Maps*, 37)

In this oddly subjective opening section Greene establishes his method: Africa as a way to know both the pain and pleasure of childhood.

The structure of the book parallels this kind of search for self knowledge. Section 1, besides serving to get Greene and his cousin out of England and onto the coast of Africa, also provides some motivation for the journey. It ends with a crucial description of "The Coast" that serves as a psychological way station on the search for a lost childhood. Section 2 plunges Greene into the "heart of darkness," both literally and psychologically. Section 3 finds Greene emerging from this darkness—both painful and pleasurable—once more into the netherworld of the coast. In this way, a literal four-week trek into the unmapped forests of Liberia also becomes a journey to discover a certain kind of darkness.

We learn in section 1 that Liberia had long attracted Greene because of its peculiar "seediness." "It seemed to satisfy . . . the sense of nostalgia for something lost; it seems to represent a stage further back" (*Maps*, 19). Greene is obsessed about this "stage further back" and returns to it again and again throughout the book. Here, in section 1, he opposes this childhood stage to the "urban stage" and reminds us that there are "a thousand names for it, King Solomon's Mines, the 'heart of darkness' if one is romantically inclined, or more simply, as Herr Heuser puts it in his African novel, *The Inner Journey*, one's place in time, based on a knowledge not only of one's present but of the past from which one has emerged" (*Maps*, 20). What all these names have in common is a "quality of darkness . . . the inexplicable. . . . an unexplained brutality" (*Maps*, 20). This brand of childhood brutality—"vivid, unselfconscious, uncorrupted"—is distinct from the urban, cerebral variety. Greene echoes Eliot by assigning to the twentieth century every kind of adult, cerebral brutality: war, revolution, materialism, and cliffs of skyscrapers. Greene makes it clear that he does not want to return to his childhood, no more than he wishes to stay in Liberia, but as he says, "when one sees to what unhappiness, to what peril of extinction centuries of cerebration have brought us, one sometimes has a curiosity to discover if one can from what we have come, to recall at which point we went astray" (*Maps*, 21).

The literal, "footsore" journey through Liberia is complicated by the incredible amount of equipment deemed necessary by European travelers early in this century. Chairs, tables, cases of whiskey, mosquito netting, hammock/chairs for carrying Greene's cousin (and Greene when he becomes ill), kitchen equipment, and tins of European food and medicine all must accompany Greene and his cousin, Barbara. These items necessitate the hiring of an equally vast amount of natives to haul them through Liberia, so that paradoxically, while Greene is traveling backward to a time of childhood innocence, he acquires the mantle of master/father over his band of carriers whom he treats as children. Greene never questions his inability to travel light, nor this curious paradox of child/father. His chief concerns are learning the way through the Liberian forest and back to the coast, keeping his carriers from deserting or quarreling among themselves, and marching 6 to 10 hours a day. Along the way he meets missionaries, prospectors, native Liberians, poverty, and illness. This literal trip, then, as Greene recognized when he returned to England, was not particularly interesting (at least not to Greene). In fact, Greene seems bored and tired most of the time. What drives the book is its insistence on the psychological observations that Greene weaves in and out of the literal trek through the Liberian forest.

The interior of this forest provides Greene with his favorite metaphor, a place where "finer terror" is palpable. This terror most often comes in the shape of a Bush Devil. These "priests" or "devils" perform religious functions in the Liberian worship ceremonies and religious dances. Apparently there are "bush schools" attended by boys and girls alike to learn the catechism of their faith. Emergence from the school signifies adulthood, and ritual scarification is then allowed. For Greene these Bush Devils, or "headmasters" as he calls them, remind him painfully of his days at public school. Elsewhere Greene has written extensively about his unhappy years as a school boy, preferring the wide open spaces of the school grounds to the terror-filled halls of rigid public school authority.[4] Greene's own childhood terrors are so bound up with public school that he identifies with the native children and their fear of the Bush Devil. "The school and the devil who rules over it are at first a terror to the child. It lies as grimly as a public school in England between childhood and manhood" (*Maps*, 90). These Bush Devils, usually the village blacksmith dressed in raffia skirts and a devil's mask with an enormous mouth, is both feared and revered. He is capable of meting out punishment but is also assigned the task of educating the young in religious mysteries. For Greene he is a powerful symbol of this childhood terror or evil, one that is not yet contaminated by the adult, cerebral variety, but which nonetheless has its own kind of power.

> One had the sensation of having come home, for here one was finding associations with a personal and a racial childhood, one was being scared by the same old witches. They brought a screaming child up to the devil and thrust him under the devil's muzzle, under the dusty raffia mane; he stiffened and screamed and tried to escape and the devil mouthed him. The older generation were playing the same old joke they had played for centuries, of frightening the child with what had frightened them. (*Maps*, 93)

One hears in this the anguish of a sensitive, fearful boy subjected to all the ritual horrors of public school initiations. This kind of terror, nameless to the boy, is what Greene seeks in Africa, "a long journey backward without maps, catching a clue here and a clue there, as I caught the names of villages from this man and that, until one has to face the general idea, the pain or the memory" (*Maps*, 97).

In order to write this book about memory, rather than Liberia, Greene foregoes a staple of the travel genre—descriptions of nature. Nineteenth-century travel writers, taking their lead from the lush descriptive passages of William Bartram and others, particularize their books with long descriptive passages devoted to the flora and fauna of a region. Mary Kingsley, it will be remembered, wrote long passages about the rivers she so loved and the forest where she learned to look. Greene's descriptions of the Liberian forest are rare, presumably because he finds it so repetitive.

> If the forest had been full of dangerous life the day's marches would have been more supportable. A few monkeys, a snake or two, the

sound of heavy birds creaking invisibly overhead, and ants, ants, everywhere, this was all the life in the dead forest. . . . It was little wonder, then, that the senses were dulled and registered only acute boredom. (*Maps*, 156–57)

Greene, ever conscious of the genre's demands, laments that other writers of Africa have represented their forests teeming with noise and life, but for him this Liberian forest does not speak in a language he knows; it is mute. A poem of A. E. Housman occurs over and over to Greene as he marches through this never-ending jungle. The poem reminds Greene of a response to nature that he had known in England. It ends, "For she and I were long acquainted / And I knew all her ways." Greene's "smash and grab raid into the primitive" (*Maps*, 119) prevents this kind of cozy British acquaintance with the land through which he marches. "It was impossible here to think of Nature in such terms of enchantment and nostalgia" (*Maps*, 158). This attitude saves Greene from oversentimentalizing nature as so many earlier writers had done or overdramatizing it so as to make their own travel accounts more splendid. Greene's account does not, however, give us any real sense of the plants and animals he encounters in Liberia. But Greene is no Peter Matthiessen; he is not by nature a man interested in the flora and fauna of his surroundings. What Greene does with this blank, dead forest is to use it as a vehicle for memory. He reminds himself that childhood is full of boredom too.

But it was only fair, I suppose, that . . . the sense that one was nearer than one had ever been to the racial source, to satisfying the desires for an instinctive way of life . . . should have been counterbalanced by the boredom of childhood too, that agonizing boredom of "apartness" which came before one had learnt the fatal trick of transferring emotion, of flashing back enchantingly all day long one's own image. . . . I sometimes wonder whether, if one had stayed longer, if one had not been driven out again by tiredness and fear, one might have relearned the way to live without transference, with a lost objectivity. (*Maps*, 158)

I take this to be a central moment for Greene on his quest for childhood's innocence and a definition of exactly what that innocence constitutes. "Transference" here must mean the exquisitely painful subjectivity that we all endure as adults, watching our-selves act and react to life's stimuli. A child has a kind of blessed objectivity; he or she is not self-conscious, does not transfer his or her own image onto the world. One comes to understand that this "racial source," this lost objectivity must be in Greene's mind responsible for the more cerebral kind of terror that adults endure and produce, rather than the more mysterious and unnamed childhood variety represented in Greene's mind by the dead dog in the pram or the witch in the hall linen closet. This passage is also an admission of Greene's failure to stay and learn the secrets of lost objectivity. Greene can only push on, racing the rainy season and his own bout with malaria. When he reaches the coast again, we learn the special role of the coast and the insights Greene has managed to gather from his gruelling march.

The Coast, neither European or African, but a "seedy" mix of both is a place that Greene particularly despises. His carriers get drunk on whisky for the first time and run into trouble with the police. Greene himself, although happy to be sleeping in a hotel room and drinking cold beer, must endure boring parties with coast officials as he awaits his boat to England. "No breaking out here, no return to something earlier, something communal, something primitive" (*Maps*, 226). Here, in Greene's psychologi-cal journey, is adolescence, neither child nor adult, but a swag-gering, self-concious kind of existence, "where we shall soon for-get the finer pleasure, the finer terror on which we might have been built" (*Maps*, 226). Even to the end, Greene is consistent with his need to define this early kind of fear and to conflate his own childhood with Africa's interior.

> This journey, if it had done nothing else, had reinforced a sense of disappointment with what man has made out of the primitive, what he had made out of childhood. . . . [T]here was something in that early terror and the bareness of one's needs, a harp strumming behind a hut, a witch on the nursery landing, a handful of kola nuts, a masked dancer, the poisoned flowers. The sense of taste was finer, the sense of pleasure keener, the sense of terror deeper and purer. (*Maps*, 225)

Greene's Africa is Greene's own childhood, a place where one can "appreciate such a beginning" (*Maps*, 249). *Journey without Maps* takes the reader to a part of Africa untouched by colonization, a feat in itself, but because of Greene's unwillingness to write a travel book that glorifies such a journey, the book is about a more difficult trip, one to the rock bottom of his consciousness, where his earliest fears are laid bare, a place, as he says in the final lines of the book, where one can see "the graves not opened yet for gold, the mine not broken with sledges" (*Maps*, 249). This subjectifying of a literal trip, an increasingly vital ingredient in the texts of Boswell, Kingsley, and Greene, would become more and more popular with later twentieth-century writers, especially V. S. Naipaul who uses India in much the same way Greene uses Africa, as a place where personal memory can be mined.

# Chapter 5

## NATURE-TRAVEL WRITING: PETER MATTHIESSEN

In her book on travel writing and imperialism, Mary Louise Pratt argues that "science and sentiment code the imperial frontier in the two eternally clashing and complementary languages of bourgeois subjectivity" (Pratt 1992, 39). For her, travel writing about the foreign and the exotic grow out of the two traditions of natural science and heroic journey. As I have noted in the introductory chapter, Pratt argues that the European concern with science and natural history begins soon after the publication of Carl Linné's *Systema Naturae* in 1735 because by then it was possible both theoretically and practically to name and classify all the plant and animal forms on the earth. The Linnaean system and its ease of classifying gave legitimacy to hundreds of expeditions from Europe to far flung parts of the globe. After this, argues Pratt, "travel and travel writing would never be the same" (Pratt 1992, 27). Travel accounts by these "naturalists" became a defining ingredient in the vast array of seafarers,' conquerors,' and adventurers' tales already available. And like these others, the naturalist conferred his (usually) male, European hegemony on the natural world. As Pratt argues, "the systemizing of nature represents not only a European discourse about non-European worlds . . . but an urban discourse about non-urban worlds, and a lettered, bourgeois discourse about non-lettered, peasant worlds" (Pratt 1992, 34). The other trend in travel writing beginning in the eighteenth century, which we have seen in Boswell's journals, is the sentimental hero as traveler. In these types of books the narrator makes himself, not nature, the center of the narrative. The paradigm is that of Ulysses's quest and journey to get home, and these travel books are full of misadventures (psychic and sexual in Boswell's case, for example), challenges, and near escapes.

In the romantic period these two strands approach one another and become dominated by the sensitivities of the narrator. Scientific writers tended to produce texts like those of Alexander von Humboldt who managed "to fuse the specificity of science with the aesthetics of the sublime" (Pratt 1992, 121). One way to aestheticize nature was to render it lush, abundant, and replete with human sentiment. Like William Bartram who had aestheticized the Americas nearly 10 years earlier, Humboldt tends to glorify the lushness of nature in human terms rather than merely to describe or name it.

> Excited by the power of light, the herbaceous Mimosa unfolds its dormant, drooping leaves, hailing, as it were, the rising sun in chorus with the matin song of the birds and the opening flowers of aquatics. Horses and oxen, buoyant with life and enjoyment, roam over and crop the the plains. (Quoted in Pratt 1992, 125)

As we have seen in Bartram and other mid-nineteenth-century travel writers, Humboldt likewise infuses a very abundant nature with human emotional qualities, in what Pratt calls a "reinventing of America." In much the same way, when nature/travel writing turns toward the sentimental and focuses on the narrator himself, we see the typical "monarch-of-all-I-survey" (Pratt 1992, 201) trope of much late-nineteenth-century travel writing.

Nature writing and travel writing, then, have never really been strangers. For that reason contemporary writers such as John McPhee, Annie Dillard, and Peter Matthiessen are claimed by both camps. But perhaps it is Peter Matthiessen alone who combines the qualities of the naturalist writer and the sentimental writer in his great book of a double journey, *The Snow Leopard*

(1978). In Matthiessen we see how a Western male naturalist both succumbs to and resists the traditional patterns that Pratt has described.

Like his other books devoted primarily to nature and science, Matthiessen's *The Snow Leopard* is on one very explicit level a scientific-travel journal in the tradition of Humboldt and Darwin. Matthiessen accompanies the zoologist George Schaller on a trek to Tibet in the fall of 1973 to help study the Himalayan blue sheep in the remote and inaccessible Dolpo region of Nepal. Matthiessen's own motivations are more complex, and they reflect the many-layered concerns of this book. One goal is to observe the elusive snow leopard which also inhabits this region and hunts the blue sheep; another is to visit the Crystal Monastery, also in the land of Dolpo, and its Buddhist lama, as elusive to the westerner as the snow leopard. A further, less tangible goal is to assuage the grief and guilt Matthiessen feels about the death of his wife.

In many ways the scientific-adventure level of the book is predictable. The trip is imperiled from the start because the travelers must go in the fall when the sheep are in rut and easily observable, but when the high passes will in some places undoubtedly be dangerous and perhaps impossible to cross. The region they have chosen to go to is extremely remote, politically unstable, hostile, and unforgiving. In the great tradition of European expeditions, they will employ porters and Sherpas who will steal and complain and desert the travelers in the worst places. *The Snow Leopard* could have been simply a traditional nineteenth-century adventure book, complete with blizzards, impassable cliffs, disgruntled porters, and daring heroism by the narrator. It could also have been, in the tradition of Alexander von Humboldt, a "reinventing" of the Himalayas according to Peter Matthiessen. To a writer more interested in Western man's ego than Matthiessen is, the temptation might have been great to describe a fierce battle between man and nature at the top of the world, to demonize nature's abundant resources and glorify man's rational success in conquering her.

Matthiessen offers these predictable elements of the naturalist-adventurer trope but manages to undermine them at the same time. In the first entry for September 28 the porters are introduced. It is typical of Matthiessen's style to make sly fun of the relationship between employer and employee. He calls Schaller and himself "sahibs" ironically in the first sentence and then goes on to describe in some detail the ethnic backgrounds of both Sherpas and porters. The Sherpas "are Buddhist herders who have come down in recent centuries out of eastern Tibet—*sherpa* is a Tibetan word for "easterner."[1] This interest in ethnicity and native language is typical of Matthiessen's more global perspective. The porters are described as "men of uncertain occupation and unsteadfast habit, notorious for giving trouble" (*Snow*, 11), but this traditional denigration of one's porter is undercut by a typical Matthiessen observation: "but it is also true that their toil is hard and wretchedly rewarded—about one dollar a day" (*Snow*, 11).

The traditional abundance-of-nature trope is also undercut by Matthiessen's grim awareness of late-twentieth-century ecology. In an early landscape passage it is to loss rather than abundance that Matthiessen draws our attention.

> Until quite recently, these Nepal lowlands were broadleaf evergreen *sal* forest (*Shorea robusta*), the haunt of elephant and tiger and the great Indian rhinoceros. Forest-cutting and poaching cleared them out. . . . The last wild Indian cheetah was sighted in central India in 1952, the Asian lion is reduced to a single small population in the Gir Forest . . . and the tiger becomes legendary almost everywhere. (*Snow*, 14)

This is a theme that both Matthiessen and Schaller are committed to: the destruction of the earth by man, and its concern dominates Matthiessen's earlier travel book about South America, *The Cloud Forest*. His concern with loss—of culture and of nature—often leads Matthiessen to invoke utopian dreams of a past "paradisal age" (*Snow*, 16) where natural abundance was possible and human interference minimal. It also literally leads him away from mankind and up into the purity of the mountains in search of a nature that is untainted. Yet even before he gets to that sacred region of Dolpo, he is ready to excise humans from the natural scene. Still in the lowlands, Matthiessen describes a landscape both devoid and full of human work.

> Awaiting the line of porters that winds through the paddies, I sit on the top level of the wall, my feet on the step on which the loads are

set and my back against a tree. In dry sunshine and the limpid breeze down from the mountains, two black cows are threshing the rice, flanks gleaming in the light of afternoon. First the paddy is drained and the rice sickled, the yoked animals, tied by a long line to a stake in the middle of the rice, are driven round and round in a slowly decreasing circle while children fling the stalks beneath their hooves. Then the stalks are tossed in the air, and the grains beneath swept into baskets to be taken home and winnowed. (*Snow*, 16)

This is a curious passage that tells much about Matthiessen's allegiances. The verbs are generally passive, no human (save the children) appear to be doing the considerable work, and "over everything lies an immortal light, like transparent silver" (*Snow*, 16). The garden is beautiful, but for Matthiessen, the people who work in it are invisible. As he moves up the trail, even these invisible people and their machines disappear, and the trekker finds himself "in the warmth and harmony and seeming plenty . . . of a paradisal age" (*Snow*, 16).

In a sense then, one might say that Matthiessen does "reinvent" the Himalayas, but in the reverse of Darwin's and Humboldt's portrait of the Americas. Instead of a strange, exotic world of lushness and plenty, Matthiessen describes a world of potential beauty, but a world that has suffered loss and degradation at the hands of man. Nonetheless, the discourse, the portrait of this Himalayan region, is still Eurocentric, male, and authoritative, and had Matthiessen only been interested in this kind of ecological polemic, the book would have been a very different one. What elevates *The Snow Leopard* to another level of travel writing is the second journey—the spiritual and emotional quest of Matthiessen himself.

What ties the two levels of the book together is the way in which Matthiessen is able finally to incorporate all that is dark and bleak about human nature into his love of nature at its "purest." Matthiessen is a Zen Buddhist, and part of the spiritual quest in this book involves Matthiessen's efforts to accept one of the basic tenets of that religion, namely the acceptance of suffering in this world. Death—of humans, of a "paradisal age"— haunts this book, and Matthiessen's incorporation of this theme into a naturalist's trek elevates *The Snow Leopard* to "a journey of the heart" (*Snow*, 3).

Matthiessen's own personal ruminations and fears about the loss of his wife are usually connected to the death and suffering he sees around him as he walks through this country. While he is still in the foothills of the greater mountains, his group passes through a small village where Matthiessen notices a small, crippled girl dragging herself along by her hands. He acknowledges her smile and her dignity and thinks of others who have suffered, including himself.

> We are subdued by this reminder of mortality. I think of the corpse in Gorkha Country, borne on thin shoulders in the mountain rain, the black cloths blowing; I see the ancient dying outside Pokhara; I hear again my own wife's final breath. (*Snow*, 22)

We learn in this intensely personal travel book that Matthiessen's wife, Deborah Love, has died six months before this trip. Because the trip takes on spiritual meaning, Matthiessen is ready not only to deal with the place of suffering in this world, but also to assess his own private suffering and its place in his life. One of the tensions of the book, aside from the traditional ones about narrow escapes and dangerous animals, is the question of whether the author can resolve his feelings of loss and emptiness. Early in the book he seems unable to. After passing the crippled child and thinking of death and suffering, Matthiessen is plagued by a sense of loss. "[S]ince the encounter with the crawling child, I look at paradise askance" (*Snow*, 24). Matthiessen seems paralyzed by and oddly attracted to the paradoxical notion that beauty is accompanied by suffering all around him. In another mountain village the beauty of the landscape "is hallucinatory—gorges and waterfalls, the pines and clouds that come and go, fire-colored dwellings painted with odd flowers and bizarre designs, the cloud-mirrors of the rice paddies in steps down the steep mountainside, a flock of vermillion minivets, blown through a wind-tossed tumult of bamboo" (*Snow*, 38). This is paradise indeed, but as they approach a village, death and suffering appear.

> At the mountain village called Sibang, to the beat of tom-toms, a buffalo is slowly killed for Durga Puja and its fresh blood drunk, while children stand in a circle in the rain. These mountain children have the big bellies of malnutrition, and though they seem no less content than the other children of the valleys, they are quiet, and do not sing out to us; one of the blood-drinkers has the loveliest face of any child that I have ever seen. (*Snow*, 38)

The clues to Matthiessen's acceptance of suffering are everywhere, but perhaps no moment is so striking as the last line of
this passage. For a Buddhist, suffering is part of life. The oneness
that Matthiessen seeks on this trip consists, in part, of accepting
suffering and death with beauty and life—the blood-drinker and
the beautiful face are one. A student of Zen Buddhism, Matthiessen knows this of course, but knowing it and living it are, as
this book describes so painfully, two very different things. Earlier
on the trip Matthiessen has admitted, "I only knew that at the
bottom of each breath there was a hollow place that needed to be
filled" (*Snow*, 43).

As the trek gets increasingly more difficult, death and suffering becomes less theoretical and more immediate. Matthiessen
and Schaller must watch every step; they must ration their food
and commit to the moment. The Zen tenet of living in the
moment is a spiritual exercise for Matthiessen that ultimately
frees him into the oneness that he seeks. On one particularly
dangerous climb along a narrow precipice, all the themes of the
book come together: nature adventure and spiritual quest inform
each other. Matthiessen is frightened by his precarious position
and horrified by his fright at the same time. Death is a reality as
he and Schaller tread carefully along a two-foot trail ("I measure
it") that drops off thousands of feet on one side. Matthiessen re-
members Buddha's teachings which say that one must "embrace
all that he most fears or finds repugnant, to better realize that
everything in the Universe, being inseparably related, is therefore holy" (*Snow*, 93). This has an effect on Matthiessen.

> Since trusting to life must finally mean making peace with death, I
> perform some mild *chod* of my own, forcing myself to look over the
> precipice whenever I can manage it. . . . It helps to pay minute atten-
> tion to detail—a shard of rose quartz, a cinnamon fern with spores, a
> companionable mound of pony dung. When one pays attention to
> the present, there is great pleasure in awareness of small things.
> (*Snow*, 93)

This Zen perspective (the sense that we can see the universe in a
grain of sand—animal, vegetable, mineral—all caught in a now
that is also forever) is a complete reversal of the traditional natu-
ralist-explorer's monarch-of-all-I-survey position. Here is Matthiessen creeping along a dangerous trail naming rocks, fern spores,

and pony dung, fearing for his life, when he could be extolling the beauty of the Himalayas that is matched in intensity only by his bravery.

These kinds of experiences instill a new acceptance in Matthiessen, and he speaks of his goals in different terms. "I would like to reach the Crystal Monastery, I would like to see a snow leopard, but if I do not, that is all right, too. In this moment there are birds" (*Snow*, 94). Even the idea of the spiritual quest takes on new meaning.

> I feel gratitude for being here, for *being*, rather, for there is no need to hie oneself to the snow mountains in order to feel free. I am not here to seek the "crazy wisdom"; if I am, I shall never find it. I am here to be here, like these rocks and sky and snow, like this hail that is falling down out of the sun. (*Snow*, 113)

In this same spirit he later cannot even tell George Schaller what he hopes to find on this trip. Neither monastery nor snow leopard seem as important as the need "to penetrate the secrets of the mountains in search of something still unknown that . . . might well be missed for the very fact of searching" (*Snow*, 126). He learns to "expect nothing" and in fact gains much.

What he gains is an entire new way of seeing and of thinking, and it is around the snow leopard that this lesson revolves. The importance of this lesson undoubtedly underlies Matthiessen's desire to name this book after that elusive animal, as much a symbol of this spiritual quest as the fabled monastery that Schaller and Matthiessen eventually reach, only to find deserted. The absence of the lama that Matthiessen had hoped to meet prepares him for his greatest discovery about the snow leopard.

The lama of the Crystal Monastery, they are told, has gone into seclusion in the mountains. Expecting nothing now, Matthiessen accidently finds the lama whom he had earlier mistaken for a crippled beggar. The unexpected gift is in itself a revelation, and he visits the lama in his cave retreat. There he asks the holy man if he is happy in his isolation.

> Indicating his twisted legs without a trace of self-pity or bitterness, as if they belonged to all of us, he casts his arms wide to the sky and the snow mountains, the high sun and dancing sheep, and cries, "Of

course I am happy here! It's wonderful! *Especially* when I have no choice! (*Snow*, 246)

This is part of the mystery of the mountains for which Matthiessen has been searching.

> In his wholehearted acceptance of *what is* . . . I feel as if he had struck me in the chest. I thank him, bow, go softly down the mountain: under my parka, the folded prayer flag glows. Butter tea and wind pictures, the Crystal Mountain, and blue sheep dancing on the snow—it's quite enough!
> Have you seen the snow leopard?
> No! Isn't that wonderful? (*Snow*, 246)

Matthiessen never does see the snow leopard, and it is upon this failure that the book's theme turns. This most difficult state of mind, the acceptance of failure or loss, is never easy for the Western psyche. As Matthiessen reminds himself, he has been programmed by his own culture to want, to desire. For such a psyche, to lose or to fail in a material quest is a saddening experience. To gain by losing, to gain something by *not* seeing the snow leopard provides Matthiessen with a perfect Zen conundrum. But, the euphoria he feels with the lama of Crystal Monastery about accepting what we have no choice about is fleeting because Matthiessen finds it difficult to take the boon of his quest home with him. Like all heroes on a quest, leaving the world that has rewarded the hero is the most difficult part of the journey. Leaving Crystal Mountain where Matthiessen can relish "nothing" proves painful, paradoxically because the *permanence* of his enlightenment is antithetical to the message of the mountains—expect nothing, accept all. Although easier physically than the northward trek to Dolpo, the way back is fraught with misgivings and depression for Matthiessen. "Far from celebrating my great journey, I feel mutilated, murderous. I am a fury of dark energies" (*Snow*, 298). This marks the low point of his journey and he says, with unconscious irony, "I look forward to nothing" (*Snow*, 298). But paradoxically, as so many moments in Zen are, this low point is also the beginning of Matthiessen's final realization.

> Already the not-looking-forward, the without-hope-ness takes on a subtle attraction, as if I had glimpsed the secret of these mountains,

still half-understood. With the past evaporated, the future pointless, and all expectation worn away, I begin to experience that *now* that is spoken of by the great teachers. (*Snow*, 300)

Once again, Matthiessen is brought back to the now. The exhilarating and dramatic journey he has just taken was not the only way to the "secret of the mountain" or the oneness with self that he so longs for. And the teacher that he sought, the lama of the Crystal Monastery, is not the only teacher on this trip.

Matthiessen has been accompanied nearly the entire way by another teacher, the enigmatic Sherpa, Tukten, although it is not until the end that Matthiessen understands Tukten's role. Initially Matthiessen is puzzled by Tukten's acceptance of a porter's duties when, as a Sherpa, he should have a higher paying and more respectable job on the expedition. During the trip, Matthiessen attributes this to Tukten's excessive drinking and foul language. Yet, the man continues to puzzle Matthiessen by his cheerful acceptance of his lowly lot and the willingness to perform any job no matter how menial. As they pass through the ethereal Himalayan landscape, Matthiessen catches Tukten smiling enigmatically, and the puzzle of this man deepens.

> I stand transfixed by this unearthly sound that radiates from all the world at once, as Tukten, passing, smiles. In this enigmatic smile there is something of Kasapa. (*Snow*, 28)

Kasapa, as we learn, is a disciple of Buddha who silently smiles in understanding when the great teacher holds up a single flower to represent the unity of existence.

Effortlessly, Tukten assumes a greater spiritual role in Matthiessen's journey. The more he is ostracized by the other Sherpas, the more Matthiessen is drawn to him.

> This disreputable fellow is somehow known to me, like a dim figure from another life. Tukten himself seems aware that we are in some sort of relation, which he accepts in a way that I cannot. . . . [His] gaze is open, calm, benign, without judgement of any kind, and yet, confronted with it, as with a mirror, I am aware of all that is hollow in myself, all that is greedy, angry, and unwise. (*Snow*, 53)

In Jungian terms, Tutken becomes Matthiessen's Shadow made visible, his painful awareness of the darker sides of himself. When

the lama of Crystal Mountain jolted Matthiessen into his acceptance of "what is," Matthiessen thought he had found his teacher.
But it is through Tukten that he discovers true acceptance of one's
complicity in pain and finds a daily practitioner of the lama's way
of life. The ever faithful Tukten has been, as Matthiessen finally
understands, his real teacher. It is Tukten's awareness of the dual
nature of human existence and his ability to live in the moment
that Matthiessen comes to see as the Sherpa's greatest lessons.

> In his life in the moment, in his freedom from attachments, in the
> simplicity of his everyday example, Tukten has taught me over and
> over, he is the teacher that I hoped to find. (*Snow*, 316)

The end of the book turns on a rendezvous arranged by Tukten
as a last meeting, but, mysteriously as ever, Tukten does not
appear. As Matthiessen circles the shrine of Bodhinath in search
of Tukten, he is left only with the smile of Kasapa and the silent
teaching of Buddha.

Matthiessen's spiritual and scientific quest, then, becomes, in
Western terms, an antiquest, mirrored by the search for Tukten at
the end. With the acceptance of loss and pain, the journey is complete. In this most peculiar of travel books, natural descriptions of
rugged and exotic landscapes are balanced by intuitive and religious mindscapes that are equally as compelling. In the end, however, this traveler cannot claim to "know" either territory. Both
remain elusive. No leopard was seen; no great tangible boon was
brought back to cure an ailing kingdom; the going was all. What
Peter Matthiessen brings back in *The Snow Leopard* is the message
that the quest does not necessarily have to involve dangerous treks
to fabled monasteries. What Tukten teaches is that our quest can
be found in life itself among its day-to-day events, both painful
and pleasurable, that make up the eternal now. Unlike Boswell,
who never quite accepts the pain and displeasure of experience,
Matthiessen finally understands the lesson of the snow leopard.

What Matthiessen offers for the travel book is further evidence
of the vitality and flexibility of the genre. Like V. S. Naipaul, his
contemporary, and Greene before him, Matthiessen's inclusion
of intensely personal information creates tensions that become
theme. More than ever, the contemporary travel book tends to be
about something more than travel, even, in the case of this book,
when travel and nature are its ostensible purposes.

Chapter 6

# "SPLENETIC TRAVELERS":
# V. S. NAIPAUL

Post-tourism travel writing, with its emphasis on inscrutability, paradox, and interrelationships, appears, perhaps grudgingly, in the early 1960s with the work of V. S. Naipaul. He represents a new kind of travel writer, a displaced exile not so much touring as wandering into, as one critic puts it, the "territory . . . of other peoples' gods where angels, anthropologists, and a liberal Western intelligentsia feared to tread."[1] Naipaul's concerns are political, social, religious, and overtly personal—the territory of contemporary travel writing. But like many of his eighteenth- and nineteenth-century predecessors, Naipaul stubbornly keeps one foot firmly in a world that calls for order and reason, while reaching toward a more modern perspective of paradox. This need for order is the ideal by which Naipaul judges the developing world in which he travels, but it is his acceptance of the paradoxical relationship of reason and unreason that exists in these countries that saves his travel books from being wholly judgmental or merely self-gratifying.

Perhaps it is Naipaul's mixed heritage that allows his unique perspective. Born in Trinidad of Indian parents and having spent most of his adult life in London, Naipaul's voice is consistently that of the outsider. His novels portray the psyches of men and women who do not fit in anywhere, whose selves cannot connect with the others around them. Most often this outsider is the exiled colonial trying to find a place in a postcolonial world. In Naipaul's novel *The Mimic Men* (1967), Ralph Singh, failed Caribbean politician living in London, is acutely aware of his own difference.[2] Yet he is unable to forge a self that does not mimic his adopted Anglo-European culture. Naipaul's novels are obsessive on this theme: the colonial has no place of his own, all is chaos for him. Not surprisingly this theme is Naipaul's own personal enigma as well and colors all his travel writing. At the beginning of his second travel book, as he sets off to discover his Indian heritage, he sounds remarkably like the tormented Singh.

> [London] had become the centre of my world and I had worked hard to come to it. And I was lost. London was not the centre of my world. I had been misled; but there was nowhere else to go.... Here I became no more than an inhabitant of a big city, robbed of loyalties, time passing, taking me away from what I was, thrown more and more into myself.[3]

Naipaul's personal journeys, like so many of those of his fictional characters, become a search for order, a search for "a resting place for the imagination" (*Area,* 29). His travel books attempt two aims at once. They reveal Naipaul himself in painful and explicitly autobiographical ways, exploring the self even more fully than does Greene. And at the same time Naipaul seeks to understand the others of India, Africa, or the Middle East. It is as though Naipaul can find a place for himself only if he resolves the problem of difference, only if he can understand where and how others differ from him. Only then will order be achieved. Yet what Naipaul finds in India is the inherent disorder of a postcolonial society that has been both improved and irreparably damaged by the years of Western dominance. This disorder mirrors the author's own sense of displacement and creates a mood of anger and gloom that pervades much of Naipaul's early travel writing. Critics from developing countries, such as George Lamming and Selwyn Cudjoe are disappointed in Naipaul's failure to rejoice in his West Indian heritage and wholeheartedly embrace the developing world. There is much justification in their objections. Yet what they miss is central to an understanding of Naipaul's bleak and even apocalyptic vision. For Naipaul, true understanding begins with the recognition of difference. True order may be a tentative dialogue between opposing forces. Naipaul is full of this kind of paradox, which celebrants of Third World autonomy resist. What for instance, do we make of Naipaul's statement "Hate oppression; fear the oppressed" (*The Mimic Men*), or an essay entitled "What's Wrong with Being a Snob?" Naipaul is not an easy writer to fully comprehend or sometimes even to like. Yet, the genius of his scrupulous observations, his fierce attachment to his subject, and his willingness to lay bare his soul have elevated and legitimized the travel book for many contemporary readers.

*An Area of Darkness* is a curiously structured book. It bears no resemblance to a traditional travel book until almost one-third of the way through. The first 90 pages offer, instead, an analysis of difference. Chapter 1, "A Resting Place for the Imagination," introduces the author and his reasons for going to India. In this highly subjective opening section, Naipaul explores his own sense of isolation and difference as a Hindu youth growing up in Trinidad. His family's isolation from the other races on the island creates in the boy a strange innocence about the matter of race. "I cannot as a child remember hearing any discussion about race. Though permeated with a sense of difference, in racial matters, oddly, I remained an innocent for long" (*Area,* 33). Even as an adult, as travel writer and novelist, Naipaul still walks a tightrope between a kind of racial innocence and an overwhelming sense of difference from other races. Undoubtedly his Brahmin upbringing accounts for much of Naipaul's estrangement from other peoples' customs and habits. "We ate certain food, performed certain ceremonies and had certain taboos; we expected others to have their own. We did not wish to share theirs; we did not expect them to share ours. They were what they were; we were what we were. . . . Everything beyond our family had this quality of difference." (*Area*, 33). As an adolescent, Naipaul ultimately rejects Hinduism as a system of belief and, as an unbeliever, he feels exiled from his own family. Yet something of the Hindu religion and his Brahmin caste survives in Naipaul the traveler, and it is that something that accounts for his hysterical reaction to India. "Examining myself, I found [remaining] only that sense of the difference of people, which I have tried to explain, a vaguer sense of caste, and a horror of the unclean" (*Area*, 35).

Naipaul moves from these intimate revelations to an assessment of his reasons for going to India. He admits to having rejected the traditions of Hinduism, yet the world and the constructs of his childhood, filled with ancient customs and sureness of difference, haunt him and draw him to India, the source of his childhood world. It is "a world which had lengthened out, its energy of inertia steadily weakening, from the featureless area of darkness which was India" (*Area*, 38). He goes to India to find that world, yet the India he finds is not a template for his childhood. In fact, Naipaul's uneasy attachment to his childhood traditions and to what they symbolize produce in him an unwilling sense of sadness whenever those traditions are threatened. "I had rejected tradition; yet how can I explain my feelings of outrage when I heard that in Bombay they used candles and electric bulbs for the Diwali festival, and not the rustic clay lamps, of immemorial design, which in Trinidad we still used?" (*Area*, 38).

This feeling of sadness and loss also generates kinship with others who are both estranged from their traditions and inextricably bound to them. Naipaul interrupts these childhood memories to tell a long story about his friendship with Ramon, the London car thief. This story provides another example of the same kind of sadness that loss of order and tradition engenders in Naipaul. It is an unlikely friendship except for the fact that Ramon is also a Hindu from Trinidad. "[W]e were debased members of that religion, and this very debasement I felt as a bond" (*Area*, 41). They are also both exiles living in London far from the Caribbean. When Ramon dies, Naipaul tries to arrange a traditional Hindu funeral, but is excluded.

> I missed Ramon's funeral. He was not cremated but buried, and a student from Trinidad conducted the rites which his caste entitled him to perform. He had read my books and did not want me to be there. Denied a presence I so much wished, I had to imagine the scene: a man in a white dhoti speaking gibberish over the corpse of Ramon, making up the rites among the tombstones and crosses of a more recent religion, the mean buildings of a London suburb low in the distance, against an industrial sky. (*Area*, 44)

Here, then, are Naipaul's themes that will emerge in his travel book about India. Traditions and their celebration of difference, no matter how lost or how obliterated by time and distance, are a source of reverence and order for Naipaul. Inevitably he finds in the modern world case after case where tradition is uprooted, debased, or even abandoned. This is the crux of Naipaul's dilemma as he travels the developing world. In India, Africa, and the Middle East he is acutely aware that there is no going back to the realm of myth and magic in which tradition is rooted, yet the shoddiness of what passes for progress in these places angers and saddens him.

But always to balance those emotions and as a way to achieve some sense of order for himself comes Naipaul's cool irony and elegant writing. Naipaul is excluded from the funeral because of his novels, which many feel are countertraditional and critical of Hindu life in Trinidad. Yet, it is Naipaul who longs for the traditional assurances of a proper burial for Ramon and the only one who cares that the rites are bogus and the setting is modern and bleak. The long, one-sentence description of the funeral, pure fiction, conveys feeling in a way no mere complaint could have. This hypersensitivity, this caring in Naipaul mitigates what could otherwise be called his conservative attachment to rigidity and structure. The entire opening chapter of *Area of Darkness,* with its long analysis of Naipaul's spiritual and philosophical background is a plea for feeling over ideology, and it is a plea to read the negative assessment of India that follows it in that light. It is what critic J. J. Healy calls "the rough ground of feeling" (Healy, 45) that Naipaul explores. It is the area of risk, the area of darkness.

The inclusion of Ramon's story, running six pages or so, folded into a 15-page chapter on Naipaul's own sense of difference and exile, itself an introduction to a travel book on India, is typical of Naipaul's narrative method. As in many travel books written after the 1960s, there is no attempt at chronology or even narrative continuity in this travel book. One recurring stylistic pattern, however, is Naipaul's expository technique which uses parts to exemplify wholes. He generalizes at length about the sadness of lost traditions, then, as an example, suddenly pulls close to Ramon in London.

> He was of a piece with the setting, the green grown dingy of the walls, the linoleum, the circles of dirt around door handles, the faded upholstery of cheap chairs, the stained wallpaper; the indications of

the passage of numberless transients to whom these rooms had never meant for the arranging of their things; the rim of soot below the windowsill, the smoked ceiling, the empty fireplace bearing the marks of a brief ancient fire and suggesting a camping ground; the carpets smelly and torn. He was of a piece, yet he was alien. (*Area*, 39)

The details of this passage—the campground effect, the indications of the dingy, transient air of the room—all clearly support Naipaul's theme of loss and disorder. The technique of describing Ramon's room rather than Ramon himself is typical of Naipaul's attention to detail and place. And, again, the clear elegance of his style, which can produce phrases like "the indications of the passage of numberless transients to whom these rooms had never been meant for the arranging of their things," becomes, as we shall shortly see, a way for Naipaul to deal with the idea of loss or, perhaps, the more plangent sense of never having belonged.

This rapid movement between exposition and description is often unsettling. One minute Naipaul is in Bombay, saddened by the electric lights, remembering Trinidad; then a few lines later he is in Ramon's room, saddened by its shabbiness and its never having been a place he could take root in, never fully occupy. But more unsettling is Naipaul's willingness to allow his ideas to contradict each other. Like many contemporary travel books, *An Area of Darkness* deepens the inscrutability of a foreign culture by the layering of mutually interfering texts. The second chapter, "Degree," contradicts the central ideas in chapter 1, where difference is celebrated and its exclusion or loss lamented. We are prepared for this change in perspective by an incident at the end of chapter 1 in which Naipaul briefly returns to the conventions of a travel book and describes his first day in Bombay.

> In Trinidad to be an Indian was to be distinctive. To be anything there was distinctive; difference was each man's attribute. To be an Indian in England was distinctive. . . . Now in Bombay I entered a shop or a restaurant and awaited a special quality of response. And there was nothing. It was like being denied part of my reality. . . . I had been made by Trinidad and England; recognition of my difference was necessary to me. (*Area*, 46)

He buys some expensive, British-made dark glasses which are mounted in cheap Indian frames. They break on the way to the hotel. He feels "less real" and retreats to his hotel "past the fat, impertinent Anglo-Indian girl, and [lies] down on [the] bed below the electric ceiling fan" (*Area*, 46). So ends chapter 1 with Naipaul in India at last, suddenly stripped of his identity, hiding even further behind defective Anglo-Indian sunglasses, exhausted from the juxtaposition of so many differences and the swallowing up of his own. The notion of inclusion and exclusion, so dear to him in Trinidad and London, now will not serve Naipaul in India.

"Degree," the chapter that follows, offers an assessment of the Indian tradition of caste, the ultimate system of difference. And it is here that we begin to witness Naipaul's own breakdown of assurances and sense of order, feelings for which he is both ashamed and still longs. It is also here that we begin to experience Naipaul's painful examination of his own feelings. Indian poverty is the first test of Naipaul's hypersensitivity. He begins with a warning to new visitors confronted by the horrors of India's starving and homeless masses. "Do not think that your anger and contempt are marks of your sensitivity.... Compassion and pity [do] not answer; they [are] refinements of hope. Fear was what I felt" (*Area*, 48). Naipaul unravels his feelings of fear by explaining the Indian concept of caste at is purest and then by following it to its most absurd extensions. Complicating this already complicated system is the influence of British rule, adding another layer of difference to a society already split by caste. In theory, says Naipaul, the caste system provides order to a chaotic society. "To define is to begin to separate oneself, to assure oneself of one's position, to be withdrawn from the chaos that India always threatens" (*Area*, 50).

This assurance of position, however, becomes absurd, as Naipaul shows in the example of the stenographer who refuses, on the grounds of caste, to type what he has taken down in shorthand. Yet this refusal arises as a result of the demands of a "modern" manager, one who operates on the British model. It is this European model that refuses to accept Indian traditions, however flawed by Western standards, and imposes systems of order of its own—its "box-wallahs," the fake, mimicked aristocracy of the colonial creature. Naipaul lays much of Indian's failure on this colonial influence, the results of which are "withdrawal, denial, confusion" (*Area*, 66). It is this confusion that the

Western traveler or travel writer might be tempted to satirize in the style of Evelyn Waugh. "The poor become faceless. Then all the rest, the dance floors, the Western mimicry, might be subjects for gentle satire" (*Area*, 71). *An Area of Darkness* is not a gentle satire. It is a book Waugh could never have written. In exposing all the systems that make up modern India—caste, British snobbery, alms-giving—Naipaul does not have a tidy picture to satirize, but rather a confusing, half-understood society that can produce in him only the feeling of fear.

This fear becomes more tangible in the third chapter called "The Colonial." This chapter has received much attention, having as its main concern human defecation. Many critics claim that Naipaul is obsessed with the subject. "The horror of the unclean" does seem to motivate much of Naipaul's interest in the yards of dung created by the Indians themselves. But it is unfair to charge him with overfastidiousness. What is more interesting is the way in which Naipaul again reverses much of what he has said in the previous chapter. Here the colonial, the outsider, is Gandhi himself, dedicated to cleaning up India as no Indian could have. Where "Degree" was critical of the colonial, this chapter offers a colonial as India's salvation. Naipaul places himself squarely on Gandhi's side but, characteristically, not without giving the Indian people their say. As a man with a sometimes uncomfortable blend of Western and Eastern values, Naipaul has a decided advantage in places like India where there is a need to see the world from both sides.

"Indians defecate everywhere." Naipaul spends much of this chapter describing in his minute way the unsanitary habits of the Indians.

> They defecate, mostly, beside the railway tracks. But they also defecate on the beaches; they defecate on the hills; they defecate on the river banks; they defecate on the streets; they never look for cover. (*Area*, 74)

Naipaul's strategy in this chapter is to intersperse these and other observations with competing views—one Eastern, one Western. The Indians "do not see these squatters;" they see themselves as clean, being required by their religion to take a bath every day, to make love with the left hand only, to take food with the right. In fact it is the existence of these very rules, designed to protect them from contamination, that allows them to ignore the heaps of dung and to use the polluted Ganges for their daily bath. This is so typical of the paradox Naipaul exposes: to cling to tradition prevents a society from entering the modern world of health and prosperity, yet abandoning these traditions creates a void at the society's center.

Gandhi's solution is simple.

> Instead of having graceful hamlets dotting the land, we have dung-heaps. . . . The one thing which we can and must learn from the West is the science of municipal sanitation. . . . A small spade is the means of salvation from a great nuisance. (*Area*, 76)

Naipaul clearly sides with Gandhi, "the failed reformer," who sees India with the eyes of an outsider. It is more than his reforms though that Naipaul admires, it is a way of seeing.

> It is possible, starting from that casual defecation in a verandah at an important assembly, to analyse the whole diseased society. Sanitation was linked to caste, caste to callousness, inefficiency and a hopelessly divided country, division to weakness, weakness to foreign rule. (*Area*, 78)

With Gandhi on his side, Naipaul proceeds to condemn Indian society, in particular the way in which the disintegration of the caste system has caused a total disintegration of meaning in India. All action has collapsed toward empty symbolism and superfluous signs. "It is the system that has to be regenerated, the psychology of caste that has to be destroyed" (*Area*, 85).

To step back and look at these three introductory chapters, as one must before continuing this curious travel book that has not traveled any farther than the mind of its author, is to be forced to assess the author's undeniable mix of emotions. One voice pleads for difference, for tradition; another condemns the system of difference. One voice laments the Indian poverty; the next voice is afraid of it. Having registered these competing emotions, Naipaul accomplishes in his travel books what he recommends to the upper-class businessmen in Bombay, cooly gossiping about India's poverty and China's impending invasion.

Express your prejudices. Say at least, "If I had the power I would do this." Say that you are on the side of this and against that. Don't just go on calmly reporting unrelated little disasters. Get angry. Get excited. Get worried. . . . Then at least I will understand. (*Area*, 65)

One suspects this would be Naipaul's advice to travel writers as well. Naipaul's passion to understand India and to have us understand India is dependent on his *not* "calmly reporting unrelated little" travel vignettes but rather analyzing, feeling, and getting angry.

Naipaul is never really comfortable in this early book with these competing feelings that India engenders in him. Like other post-tourism travel writers that follow him, he presents competing texts that offer an open view, yet, unlike his followers, this travel writer clearly longs for order and stasis. In his book *Paradoxes of Order*, Robert Morris recognizes this same uneasiness in Naipaul's fictional characters. In this case it is "the rootless protagonist's movement from an almost supernal innocence to moments of self-doubt and/or disgust when the wellspring of illusion is poisoned, when past and expectations of the future are annihilated by the 'free' act that shatters both will and desire."[4] What happens in Naipaul's own autobiographical travel books as well as in his characters' minds is that freedom and order compete. As Morris rightly says, Naipaul constantly asks in his early novels, "can one in 'a free state,' in the primal condition of exile, really discriminate between chaos and order at all; and if not, what happens to a man when his perceptions of them totally break down?" (Morris, 75). This is exactly the same question that Naipaul the traveler asks about postcolonial countries (and himself), exiled from both their own past and their colonial masters, free, but perched on the brink of chaos. For Naipaul himself the answer is a kind of detachment that ironically allows him to travel in places that so move him to anger and sorrow. This detachment becomes clearer in the final two sections of *An Area of Darkness* as Naipaul uses his own encounters in India as examples of the general assumptions he has wrestled with in part 1.

The issue of colonial rule, so detested by Naipaul as the source of India's problems, is presented on a microlevel in the Dal Lake section of part 2. In this northern resort area, far from the teeming mobs of Bombay, Naipaul rents a room in the nearly empty Hotel Liward and prepares for a lengthy stay. During this time he develops a master-servant relationship with the illiterate and wily Aziz. As Naipaul penetrates his own insecurity in this relationship, we begin to see on a small scale what had happened to India during the years of British rule. Ironically, of course, it is Naipaul who plays the part of the Western master, and it is the ability to detach himself even from his own beliefs that makes the section remarkable. Incident after incident with Aziz produces the same result. The servant is placed in a position of having to both cater to and outwit the master, losing himself in the bargain. Aziz is completely defined by his servant role. Naipaul, in turn, is made to look ridiculous. In scenes like the one following, Naipaul is able to dissociate himself from his own status in order to show the painful insecurity of the ruling class.

> This was the price of Aziz's intercession. Had they come to some arrangement of the previous afternoon? Had it been planned some days before? Had Aziz intended all his groans and complaints to lead to this, an extra five rupees? . . . He seemed surer of me: He had taken a gift—in the long run my money—in my presence. Throughout the journey he had promoted my dignity; he must have frightened the *ghora-wallah* with my importance. But this true assessment was plain. I was harmless. Faced with this assessment, I felt my will weaken. (*Area*, 183)

The paradox of order continues. Naipaul seeks out an "orderly" servant-master relationship designed to give him the most freedom. But, like Aziz, he too is trapped inside this same system, one he doesn't quite understand.

In the final section, toward which the book has been inevitably moving, Naipaul begins his much-delayed trip to the village of his grandfather. The detachment Naipaul feels when he visits the village of the Dubes is mirrored in language both sure and painful. The pain is a result of Naipaul's illusion that he will find some identity here, some resemblance between himself and the people of his grandfather's village. What he finds instead is a difference so broad he cannot breach it. Expectation and reality are too far apart for Naipaul. The chief's house is a thatched hut amid other more prosperous brick houses; the old woman's story about Naipaul's grandfather moves him only to give her money; the old photographs are not comforting.

> Photographs were then brought out, as old to me and as forgotten as the images; and it was again disturbing to my sense of place and time to handle them, to see, in the middle of a vast land where I was anchored to no familiar points and could so easily be lost, the purple stamp of the Trinidad photographer—his address so clearly pictured—still bright against the fading sepia figure, in my reawakened memory forever faded, belonging to imagination and never to reality like this. (*Area*, 270)

The tension here between order and chaos, between belonging and not belonging, between memory and reality, are the same themes that hold *An Area of Darkness* together. Whether Naipaul is arguing about India or himself, the same crosscurrents emerge, pulling both man and country apart.

In this early travel book the tension is never really resolved. *An Area of Darkness* ends with a scene that contains all of these crosscurrents painfully exposed by Naipaul. After being pestered by the village elders to intercede in an old legal dispute, Naipaul leaves his grandfather's village in a frenzy of disappointment and is deliberately cruel to a young boy who begs for a ride.

> Too much had been assumed; I felt overwhelmed; I wished to extricate myself at once.
>
> "Shall we take him on?" the IAS man asked, nodding towards the boy.
>
> "No. Let the idler walk."
>
> We drove off. I did not wave. The headlamps of the jeep shot two separate beams into the day's slowly settling dust which made turbulent again by our passage, blotted out the scattered lights of the village.
>
> So it ended, in futility and impatience, a gratuitous act of cruelty, self-reproach and flight. (*Area*, 277)

This mood settles on the end of the book. Naipaul ends with the judgment: "It was a journey that ought not to have been made; it had broken my life in two" (*Area*, 280). Yet Naipaul's failure is not the book's failure. The gap between what Naipaul wants for his text and what the text actually does governs both the tone and meaning of the book. *An Area of Darkness* ends with a dream

Naipaul has upon returning to London with the gift of some Indian cloth to be cut into a jacket. The dream, about this cloth, gives us some insight into Naipaul's agony about his experience.

> An oblong of stiff new cloth lay before me, and I had the knowledge that if only out of this I could cut a smaller oblong of specific mea-surements, a specific section of this cloth, then the cloth would begin to unravel of itself, and the unravelling would spread from the cloth to the table to the house to all matter, *until the whole trick was undone.* Those were the words that were with me as I flattened out the cloth and studied it for the clues which I knew existed, which I desired above everything else to find, but which I knew I never would. (*Area*, 280)

The desire here to know everything, to unravel knowledge by cutting an orderly oblong is so revealing. On the one hand, Naipaul seems to sense that knowledge is a process of unravel-ing, the coming-apart-at-the-seams kind of experience that we have when reading *An Area of Darkness.* Yet he longs for the orderly oblong and the clues that will help him cut it. It is through this "paradox of order" that the reader finds meaning where Naipaul finds pain.

The struggle that Naipaul feels about his travel writing lies just where the genre itself starts to change. Naipaul is a figure who can both represent the heyday of the travel book with its elegant writing and deep introspection, and also suggest where the travel book is going—toward paradox, inscrutability, and openness.

Chapter 7

# "LYING TRAVELERS": BRUCE CHATWIN

The most persistent characteristic of late-twentieth-century travel writing is the refusal of the authors to admit to knowing anything for sure. There is a mood of off-centeredness in the books of these writers, as if, through the experiences of travel, certainties have been displaced and made as strange as the land through which the writers journey. As we have seen, this off-centeredness in Naipaul's writing is an unwilling one; it comes more from the paradoxes inherent in his work than from his own convictions. In Matthiessen's work, we follow the author's painful, daily uncertainties about himself and the modern world. What results from travel books like these is not smooth narratives that purport to deliver the truth about another culture, but rather, as anthropologist James Clifford says, "a series of specific dialogues, impositions, and inventions."[1] These "impositions and inventions" would seem antithetical to a work of documentary "fact" like a travel book, but more and more travel writers are crossing that line between fact and fiction and becoming what Laurence Sterne called "Lying Travelers." The travel writer most attuned to this odd perspective is the idiosyncratic Bruce Chatwin. His two "travel books," *In Patagonia* (1977) and *The Songlines* (1987), may not even be travel books at all but, instead, meditations on the contradictions of travel itself. His own "dialogues, impositions, and inventions" obliterate the divisions, not only between fact and fiction, but also between wandering and dwelling. Chatwin's contribution to the genre may in fact be to stretch its limits to the breaking point. In fact, he always vigorously resisted the term *travel book* for his work.

Before his early death at age 47 in 1989, Chatwin's obsessive theme in both his life and his work was the tug-of-war between human restlessness and acquisitiveness, between the urge to wander and the urge to settle and collect. Chatwin's life embodied both extremes. As a young man in his twenties, Chatwin worked at Sotheby's in London, becoming an expert collector. But, as Chatwin tells the story, one day he woke up blind; his doctor recommended wider horizons. Regardless of whether this story is real or apocryphal, Chatwin quit his job in the art world and became an inveterate wanderer, preferring the dry places, going "alone, travelling light."[2] Yet, he never really stopped collecting. His books are compendiums of portraits, encyclopedias of ideas. How he resolves the apparent differences between collecting and wandering, and how he manages to create a dialogue between those who stay and those who go are central to his vision as an entirely original travel writer.

The story of Cain and Abel appears in both *The Songlines* and *In Patagonia* because it so perfectly encapsulates the motifs of dwelling and wandering, crime and expiation, and the nomad and the farmer—thematic motifs that Chatwin returns to again and again. In the "Notebooks" section of *The Songlines*, where Chatwin collects his encyclopedic texts on the nature of human restlessness, the story of the two brothers receives several interpretations. All versions turn on the idea of "the envy of the prisoner for the freedom of open spaces" (*Songlines*, 93). Cain, the settled farmer, kills Abel, the wandering shepherd, and is ironically condemned to mark his crime by traveling east of Eden where Abel once traveled before him. In Chatwin's books, then, wandering is associated with restlessness, creativity, and passionate crime. The settler is associated with envy, greed, and warfare. Chatwin explores these associations further as he ponders the etymological roots of the two brothers' names.

The names of the brothers are a matched pair of opposites. Abel comes from the Hebrew *"hebel,"* meaning "breath" or "vapour": anything that lives and moves and is transient, including his own life. The root of "Cain" appears to be the verb *"kanah":* to "acquire," "get," "own property," and so "rule" or "subjugate." (*Songlines,* 193)

The connection between collecting and ruling is essential to Chatwin's understanding of the difference between the nomad and the settler. In our world, dominated as it is by those who have settled, possessions are seen as a way to insulate the self from the other. James Clifford makes this same point in his study of the connections between art and ethnology. Like Chatwin, he argues that "in the West . . . collecting has long been a strategy for the deployment of a possessive self, culture, and authenticity" (Clifford, 218). Chatwin's point is that the Western ideal of a self who is an owner has dominated the world's values and thereby subjugates the alternative of a self or a culture that wanders, "travelling light."

The twin ideas of moving and staying, of incompletedness and completion dominate Chatwin's work. Although he clearly favors movement, he understands that neither pole is sufficient alone, that a precious kind of energy is produced at the meeting ground of these two powerful forces. As Clifford reminds us, authenticity or purity of position is no longer possible in the contemporary mix of cultures. The nomadic Masai are forced to settle because of Kenya's extensive park system. The Chicago businessperson, at home in the suburbs, is forced to travel relentlessly to meet with his or her international counterparts. Yet this fusion of opposites need not be a source of anxiety. As Clifford explains, "culture and identity are inventive and mobile. They need not take root in ancestral plots; they live by pollination, by (historical) transplanting" (Clifford, 15). In the dialogue between wandering and settling, loss of purity can mean recovery of energy.

The exile knows this compromise best. *In Patagonia* is full of characters who, like Cain, are exiles, living out their dreams between restlessness and resettlement. And like Cain who dreamed of the new city he would build, these exiles from Wales or Spain or Chile, or even the indigenous Indians exiled from their own land carry with them illusions of a pure and ideal life that never quite materializes in Patagonia. Chatwin, too, begins his trip to Patagonia with a dream. The book opens with this memory.

> In my grandmother's dining-room there was a glass-fronted cabinet and in the cabinet a piece of skin. It was a small piece only, but thick and leathery, with strands of coarse, reddish hair. It was stuck to a card with a rusty pin. On the card was some writing in faded black ink, but I was too young then to read.
> "What's that?"
> "A piece of brontosaurus."
> My mother knew the names of two prehistoric animals, the brontosaurus and the mammoth. She knew it was not a mammoth. Mammoths came from Siberia.
> The brontosaurus, I learned, was an animal that had drowned in the Flood, being too big for Noah to ship aboard the Ark. I pictured a shaggy lumbering creature with claws and fangs and a malicious green light in its eyes. Sometimes the brontosaurus would crash through the bedroom wall and wake me from my sleep.
> This particular brontosaurus had lived in Patagonia, a country in South America, at the far end of the world. Thousands of years before, it had fallen into a glacier, travelled down a mountain in a prison of blue ice, and arrived in perfect condition at the bottom. Here my grandmother's cousin, Charley Milward the Sailor, found it.[3]

This opening passage reveals not only the germ of Chatwin's quest but also the themes he will explore in his first travel book. His ostensible reason for traveling to Patagonia is to recover another piece of the skin. The original, part of his grandmother's collection of personal momentos and so precious to Chatwin as a boy, had long been discarded as trash after his grandmother's death. But by that time Patagonia had already become a kind of magic land to Chatwin. As he says, "My interest in Patagonia survived the loss of the skin" (*Patagonia*, 3). During the Stalin era, the Chatwin family dreams of sailing to Patagonia to escape the "Cannibal of the Kremlin." "Stalin died," writes Chatwin, "but I continued to hold Patagonia in reserve" (*Patagonia*, 3). Like most of the people he eventually meets there, Patagonia becomes for Chatwin a land where dreams can be fulfilled.

The tension between science and myth, between illusion and reality that informs the rest of the opening section prepares us for a Patagonia where dreams collide with reality, where fiction speaks to history. His mother's version of the beast, the Bible story, and a kind of mixture of the two where the "brontosaurus" travels in a "prison of blue ice" into the hands of Charley Milward are all treated with equal interest by Chatwin. As a school boy these stories are challenged for the first time when they meet the stories that science has to offer.

> At school they laughed at the story of the brontosaurus. The science master said I'd mixed it up with the Siberian mammoth. He told the class how Russian scientists had dined off deep-frozen mammoth and told me not to tell lies. (*Patagonia*, 2)

The tension here between the boy's "lies" and those of the science teacher is consistent with Chatwin's open view of "truth." Even though the young boy becomes confused and "ashamed," the adult Chatwin never quite chooses between myth and science. When he researches the origin of the skin, he is still able to tread a middle ground between the two that will color the entire book.

> It took some years to sort the story out. Charley Milward's animal was not a brontosaurus, but the mylodon or Giant Sloth. He never found the whole specimen, or even the whole skeleton, but some skin and bones, preserved by the cold, dryness and salt, in a cave on Last Hope Sound in Chilean Patagonia. He sent the collection to England and sold it to the British Museum. This version was less romantic but had the merit of being true. (*Patagonia*, 3)

Although truth clearly has some value here for Chatwin, the scientific explanation of the mylodon seems to remain another, less romantic version of the story. Chatwin is fascinated with different versions of stories, some of which may or may not have the merit of being true. Patagonia seems to be a place that is full of competing stories.

One of these is the legend of Butch Cassidy and the Sundance Kid, a typical Patagonian history. Its protagonists are wanderers, collecting other peoples' money as they go. They flee to Patagonia as a last refuge with dreams of building a new life. Their violent death there is characteristic of other exiles' disillusion with a Patagonian dream that does not come true. But as Chatwin traces this story in and out of several chapters, through miles of Patagonian wasteland, he discovers many different versions of the outlaws' fate. The popular account of their death, a shootout in San Vicente, Bolivia, in December 1909, is traced to a poet named Chapman.

> No one knows where Chapman got the story: Butch Cassidy could have invented it himself. His aim, after all, was to "die" in South America and re-emerge under a new name. The shooting at San Vicente was investigated by the late President René Barrientos, Ché Guevara's killer, himself an ardent Western history buff. He . . . concluded that the whole thing was a fabrication. (*Patagonia*, 49)

Chatwin, himself an ardent collector of "truths," later goes to Utah to visit Cassidy's sister who swears she ate blueberry pie with her brother in the fall of 1925. Chatwin travels through Patagonia to find other people with different versions of this same story. His research results in a Borges-like picture of history where fact competes with fact. The mystery is never resolved. Like the other stories Chatwin finds in Patagonia, the legend of Butch Cassidy and the Sundance Kid exists somewhere in the crosscurrents between dream and history.

The Patagonia that Chatwin discovers as he walks its length and breadth is an ideal setting for an exile's dream. Its bleak, featureless landscape becomes a kind of *tabula rasa* for a new life. Its openness to foreign exiles and their hopes creates a kind of cross-cultural mix that is at times surreal. Chatwin has an eye for this kind of cultural cross-fertilization in the details of place. At a Welsh settlement he discovers dreams and reality, both foreign and indigenous, in a curious blend. Port Madryn had been settled in 1865 by 153 desperate Welsh colonists.

> They were poor people in search of a New Wales, refugees from cramped coal-mining valleys, from a failed independence movement, and from Parliament's ban on Welsh in schools. Their leaders had combed the earth for a stretch of open country uncontaminated by Englishmen. They chose Patagonia for its absolute remoteness and foul climate. (*Patagonia*, 24)

Instead of a New Wales, Chatwin finds "a town of shabby concrete buildings, tin bungalows, tin warehouses and a wind-flattened garden" (*Patagonia*, 21). The land is still characterized by its "absolute remoteness." But Chatwin captures the overlay of dream upon reality in the description of that landscape.

> I walked along the esplanade and looked out at the even line of cliffs spreading round the bay. The cliffs were a lighter grey than the grey of the sea and sky. The beach was grey and littered with dead penguins. Halfway along was a concrete monument in memory of the Welsh. It looked like an entrance to a bunker. Let into its sides were bronze reliefs representing Barbarism and Civilization. Barbarism showed a group of Tehuelche Indians, naked with slabby back muscles in the Soviet style. The Welsh were on the side of Civilization—greybeards, young men with scythes, and big-breasted girls with babies. (*Patagonia*, 22)

In this passage, the heroic fiction of the civilized westerner dominating the brute native is mitigated by the bleakness of Patagonia. In the gray setting neither civilization nor barbarism prevails, only a kind of entropy. As he turns away from this scene and enters a restaurant, Chatwin describes a more lively collection of fictions barely less entropic than the landscape yet somehow capable of surviving.

> At dinner the waiter wore white gloves and served a lump of burnt lamb that bounced on the plate. Spread over the restaurant wall was an immense canvas of gauchos herding cattle into an orange sunset. An old-fashioned blonde gave up on the lamb and sat painting her nails. An Indian came in drunk and drank through three jugs of wine. His eyes were glittering slits in the red leather shield of his face. The jugs were of green plastic in the shape of penguins. (*Patagonia*, 22)

Here the green plastic penguins, the orange sunset of the gauchos, the glittering eyes of the Indian, and the white gloves of the hopeful waiter contrast with what is outside the restaurant—the gray deadness of Patagonia. Survival in a place like Port Madryn may depend on the colorful fictions and the incongruous mixtures that dominate the room. The blonde representative of civilization is clearly not isomorphic with the big-breasted, fertile women of the Welsh dreams; neither is the Indian particularly brutal. They share a common boredom. Dreams may not come true in Patagonia, but its nonessentialist landscape is a place where the process of loss is balanced, however strangely, with the process of recovery.

The loss of illusions is harder on some Patagonians than others. The book is filled with stories of those who recover and those who don't. The most successful seem to blend dream with reality—fiction with fact. One "perfect English gentleman" Chatwin meets is dressed in tweed, khaki, and tortoiseshell but is married to a Spanish woman and cannot remember where Gloucestershire is. The Texan, Martin Sheffield, on the other hand, comes to Patagonia in the 1920s believing it to be an extension of the Old West. He stubbornly plays out his dreams of being a sheriff and a crack shot, "picking off ladies' high-heeled shoes" (*Patagonia*, 39), but dies of "gold fever, starvation, and the D.T.'s" (*Patagonia*, 40). Patagonia seems to be a place where the unpacking of an exile's dreams is at least partially essential to his establishment of a new life there.

In Chatwin's version of Patagonia, every person drawn to that remote part of Argentina and Chile has lived a life on the borderline between wandering and collecting. From Charles Darwin, who sails off for years in the *Beagle* to collect specimens, to Charley Milward gathering mylodon skin in a cave, Patagonia attracts them. Indeed, Chatwin suggests that not only were these more traditional travelers attracted to Patagonia's blank canvas, but also writers such as Shakespeare, Coleridge, and Poe were drawn to the mysterious meeting place that is Patagonia. This rather free mingling of history and literature, juxtaposing mariner's tales with Poe and Shakespeare, has a curious effect on the tone of the book. This is certainly no ordinary travel book replete with bad train trips, scurrilous guides, and sorry food. One is never quite sure, in fact, whether Chatwin has actually conjured up these incredible characters to accommodate some literary ideas of his own.

Inviting fiction into a travel narrative, however, is to invite a certain amount of scorn. Chatwin found his own friends and fellow travel writers, highly skeptical. In a 1989 interview with Paul Theroux at the Poetry Center in New York City, the subject of note taking arose. In an answer to George Plimpton's question about note taking in the field, Theroux said that he didn't take notes, but "worked hard at getting the gist of what happened." This statement clearly jogged his memory about his late friend Bruce Chatwin, and he continued.

My friend Bruce Chatwin didn't write like that at all. He really didn't believe in a "travel book." I said to him about *In Patagonia* that "you say what it's like but you don't say how you get from place to place." Chatwin said, "You have to embroider." Actually he invented characters. He said to me, "I don't believe in coming clean, do you?"[4]

This refusal to "come clean," to side with truth or fiction, myth or history may have been a habit of mind for Chatwin that enabled him to write travel books that exist on the borderline between document and fiction. The story of the illness that killed him could have been culled from one of his books. "I had . . . picked up a very rare fungus of the bone marrow in China."[5] This story is usually qualified by other writers with phrases like, "he told friends"[6] or "what he described as,"[7] because of the likelihood that he died of AIDS.[8] Whatever the source of his gift, the Patagonian stories he collects are about how fictions drive people to wander and how fictions sustain them in hostile, unfriendly places.

*The Songlines*, a more polemic book than *In Patagonia*, is also more obviously a work of fiction. Indeed, after publication, Chatwin fought with his editor to have the book labeled fiction instead of nonfiction. It is really a blending of both in a kind of anatomy of travel. The framework on which the ideas hang is a picaresque tale of a man named Arkady Volchok whom Chatwin meets in Australia on his quest to understand the mysteries of the Aboriginal Songlines. The story of Chatwin and Arkady traveling through the desert to help reestablish the land rights of the Aboriginals by listening to their Songlines or Dreamings is interwoven with Chatwin's own notebooks for his lifelong project on nomadism. *The Songlines* is an attempt to answer Chatwin's "question of questions: the nature of human restlessness . . . why greener pastures pall on us; why possessions exhaust us, and why Pascal's imaginary man found his comfortable lodging a prison" (*Songlines*, 161–62).

As Chatwin himself explains, to accomplish this task he "decided to write an imaginary dialogue in which both narrator and interlocutor had the liberty to be wrong" ("Quartet," 50) We sense that the interlocutor, Arkady, is imaginary as well in dialogues like this one.

> "To wound the earth" [Arkady] answered earnestly, "is to wound
> yourself, and if others wound the earth, they are wounding you. The
> land should be left untouched: as it was in the Dreamtime when the
> Ancestors sang the world into existence."
> "Rilke," I said, "'had a similar intuition. He also said song was exis-
> tence."
> "I know," said Arkady, resting his chin on his hands. "'Third Son-
> net to Orpheus.'" (*Songlines*, 11)

The rough, Australian-born Arkady, driving his Land Rover over
the Australian outback, sounds remarkably like Chatwin's alter
ego trading subtleties of Rilkean poetry. But *The Songlines* is not an
ordinary travel book; it is not even a Chatwinian travel book in the
same way that *In Patagonia* is. Despite the requisite descriptive passages of reddish, rocky Australia and meetings with "native infor-
mants," *The Songlines* is primarily a book of ideas; it is a dialogue
between the interchangeable Chatwin and Arkady, and between
the reader and a collection of ideas. And one finds that the central
metaphor of the Aboriginal notion of singing the world into existence allows this travel book to cross the line into fiction.

The concept of the Songlines is complex. Aboriginal creation
myths tell of a period known as the Dreamtime, when gigantic
beings burst from the center of the new earth and wandered over
Australia singing out the name of everything that crossed their
path. They left a trail of words and musical notes along the way,
marking their Dreaming-tracks. As Arkady explains,

> In theory, at least, the whole of Australia could be read as a musical
> score. There was hardly a rock or creek in the country that could not
> or had not been sung. One should visualize the Songlines as a
> spaghetti of Iliads and Odysseys, writhing this way and that, in which
> every "episode" was readable in terms of geology. (*Songlines*, 13)

The idea of a nomad creating a world through his own words as
he walked through the dry places must have been enormously
appealing to Chatwin. Both *In Patagonia* and *The Songlines* are
attempts to do this same thing, to create a world for the reader
blending fiction, nonfiction, history, and myth. So the rather
flimsy narrative of Arkady and Chatwin is only a vehicle to explain the system of the Songlines and to frame the notes that
Chatwin has collected on the theme of nomadism.

These notebooks occupy nearly one-third of the book, and their sources range from quotes cribbed from Baudelaire and Rimbaud, to travel stories, to Chatwin's own studies in linguistics, archeology, and anthropology. His thesis is no mystery: Chatwin clearly favors the nomadic life, and *The Songlines* is more concerned with the Aboriginal nomad as metaphorical object than as ethnographic subject. In Chatwin's last travel book we have come so far from the traditional, even modern, travel book. Theme, or what the book is about is the primary concern here. Sights and people met may be imaginary; they exist to support the book's thesis. And the thesis is that the nomadic life may offer alternatives for the settlers of the world. The notebooks offer quotes such as these to support that claim.

> Psychiatrists, politicians, tyrants are forever assuring us that the wandering life is an aberrant form of behaviour; a neurosis; a form of unfilled sexual longing; a sickness which, in the interests of civilization, must be suppressed.

> Nazi propagandists claimed that gipsies and Jews—peoples with wandering in their genes—could find no place in a stable Reich.

> Yet, in the East, they still preserve the once universal concept: That wandering re-establishes the original harmony which once existed between man and the universe. (*Songlines*, 178)

> Natural Selection has designed us—from the structure of our brain-cells to the structure of our big toe—for a career of seasonal journeys *on foot* through a blistering land of thorn-scrub desert. (*Songlines*, 162)

Chatwin's books, which neither romanticize nor glorify the nomad and the exile, do offer a nomadic option of reading the world as text, of collecting signs instead of truths, where interpretation of those signs is defined as an ongoing process that preserves at all times "the liberty to be wrong." Like the Aboriginals he so admires (or his construct of them), Chatwin prefers to admit to singing the world into existence—be it Patagonia's world or Australia's. Claims to truth and power are inconsequential in the kind of travel writing where wandering is "one continuous act of creation" (Buruma, 100).

## Chapter 8

# ENVOI: WRITINGS OF PLACE AND THE POETICS OF DISPLACEMENT IN THE WORKS OF PAUL THEROUX AND ROLAND BARTHES

Travel writing, like other writings of place—nature writing or the war memoir, has long felt its prerogative to be the representation of place, to fix in our minds the contours and colors of a particular region of the globe. As Dennis Porter observes in *Haunted Journeys*, "Such representations are always concerned with the question of place and of placing, of situating oneself once and for all vis-a-vis an Other or others" (Porter, 20). The blind authority with which an observer situates himself among others and then commits to narrative the characteristics of that place and its people can create what Mary Louise Pratt calls "othering."

> The people to be othered are homogenized into a collective "they," which is distilled even further into an iconic "he." ... The portrait of manners and customs is a normalizing discourse, whose work is to codify difference, to fix the Other in a timeless present where all "his" actions and reactions are repetitions of "his" normal habits. Thus, it

textually produces the Other without an explicit anchoring either in the observing self or in a particular encounter in which contact with the Other takes place.[1]

This study has suggested that if we look back on the several hundred years of travel writing with an eye to this kind of authority and distancing between observer and observed, we can see an evolution of concern with the problems of representing the other fairly. The crisis of this concern, having made its way from the consciousness of those foreign cultures being represented to the more exotic world of literary criticism, is a relatively contemporary one. As Edward Said reminds us in his article "Representing the Colonized," the whole issue of representation is seen as problematical in the late twentieth century. Essence and truth are no longer stable qualities that can be drawn, described, or symbolized through language. Hence, the art of representing a place or a group of people is currently seen to be a dubious effort at best and an act of "hegemonic discourse" at worst. Despite (or perhaps because of) these waverings, contemporary travel writing still flourishes. But the most culturally sensitive kind of travel writing has wrestled with the complexities of self and other and made that its subject.

As we have seen, Bruce Chatwin's two travel books provide models for experimenting with the genre. Walking and talking his way through foreign countries, Chatwin maintains an ongoing dialogue with the world's citizens about the nature of human restlessness. His assumption that we are all at heart exiles connects him to those he meets as he walks their roads and stays in their homes. His preference for wandering in the dry places allies him with the nomadic heritage of permanent displacement. If, as Dennis Porter has said, "centeredness is a myth that sustains all our other myths" (Porter, 303), then Chatwin's ability to be decentered or displaced accounts for his open-ended attitude toward not only foreign cultures but truth and history as well. The acceptance of being off center places one in a position of ignorance and doubt; nothing is sure. If our familiar constructs and sustaining myths can be left at home like Chatwin's very British life, then a world traveler is less likely to import judgmental convictions as he encounters those who are different. Like the nomad, he can travel light.

Despite the experimental efforts of Chatwin and, to some extent, Matthiessen and Naipaul, the duality of self and other still haunts most travel writers. Not all representations of place can escape the centering within the narrative that leads to othering. One of the most popular travel writers today, whose name is practically synonymous with contemporary travel writing, Paul Theroux, is a good example of a prolific and entertaining writer who opts for the most traditional and potentially othering convention of the travel genre: the panorama.

As Pratt reminds us in her essays and her recent study of travel writing, *Imperial Eyes*, to describe a foreign landscape or city using a panoramic view betrays a tendency toward dominance and imperialism. "In contemporary travel accounts, the monarch-of-all-I-survey scene gets repeated, only now from balconies of hotels in big third-world cities" (Pratt 1992, 216). Pratt contrasts Theroux's grumpy descriptions of Guatemala with the "sparkling panoramas" of Burton and Humboldt to show that despite their antithetical messages, Theroux is nonetheless still imposing Western values on the scene he surveys from the relative safety and privacy of his hotel balcony. Guatemala is not the only example. In *The Old Patagonian Express*, Theroux, sick of the altitude and the poverty of Peru, retreats to his hotel room above the plaza and surveys the scene below him.

> There were lights on in the plaza. The leper I had seen that afternoon shuffling on bleeding feet, like the Pobble who had no toes, was curled up near the fountain. On the far side was the beautiful Jesuit church, and beyond that the Andes as black and high-crowned as the hats of the Indians who were also bunking down in the plaza.[2]

From his vantage place above the inhabitants of the plaza, Theroux has a kind of luxury he does not have during the day when he must deal with the leper and the Indians whose hats he does not understand. From his hotel window the leper and the Indians are reduced to types: the leper is animal-like, "curled up near the fountain;" the Indians become associated only with the black hats that are their exotic cultural markers and with the distant mountains from where they came. The choice of the phrase *bunking down* further distances the Indians through Theroux's smug humor and aligns these homeless Indians with a Boy Scout camping trip. The

Jesuit church, in contrast, is "beautiful." Instead of lush beauty, Theroux finds ugliness and disorder. Where Humboldt, Burton, and others imbued their landscapes with meaning, Theroux finds emptiness, meaninglessness, and "semantic underdevelopment" (Pratt, 218). But like the eighteenth- and nineteenth-century travelers, by the act of judging—awarding value—Theroux continues to dominate the scene.

When compared to Chatwin's version of Patagonia, which is teeming with exiles and storytellers to the last line, Theroux's Patagonia seems strangely empty and quiet.

> The Patagonian paradox was this: to be here, it had helped to be a miniaturist, or else interested in enormous empty spaces. There was no intermediate zone of study. Either enormity of the desert space, or the sight of a tiny flower. You had to choose between the tiny or the vast. (*Express*, 476–77)

A foreign place as a "zone of study" betrays Theroux's position as one who, despite his humor and, at times, self-effacement, remains a traditional travel writer wholly centered within his narrative and positionally capable of the imperialist and othering tropes that are part of the genre's heritage. Pratt calls this stylistic position "the rhetoric of presence" (Pratt 1992, 204). The author is wholly centered within the narrative, and, as in both travel writing and anthropology, these narratives say more about the author than they do about the people described.

Yet, a nagging question remains about the nature of the travel book. Is it possible to absolutely decenter oneself as narrator? Is the "poetics of displacement" (Clifford, 10)—the radical unpacking of our cultural baggage by travel writers—entirely possible? Is there no way can we ever know the other? Roland Barthes, a proponent of extreme displacement in his travel book *Empire of Signs* (1970),[3] argues that no knowledge is possible and perhaps not even desirable. The book, as Dennis Porter rightly argues, is "antihermeneutical." No meaning is achieved; Barthes offers no reading of the text that is Japan. Barthes's book is a prescient answer to Edward Said's *Orientalism* (1978), a later work that challenged all Western ethnological writing by charging that it othered, in Pratt's sense, an entire region of the world, its people, and their history. Said shares with Foucault a suspicion of knowing others, since for both men knowledge is aligned with power. Those who wield power in this world set up the rules by which those who do not have power are known. Barthes offers a model in *Empire of Signs* that does not yearn for knowledge but skates along the surface of its own perceptions. But, as Edmund White remarks in his review of the book, Barthes's Japan suits his own semiotic agenda. "If Japan did not exist, Barthes would have had to invent it."[4]

Everything that Barthes finds in Japan—the theater, the haiku, the food—is beyond interpretation. Take apart a haiku and there is nothing but the surface image. Like the incredibly elaborate Japanese package, the contents of Japanese cultural icons are not meant to be unwrapped. It is the "beguiling surface" that matters. This clearly appeals to Barthes; it is "paradise, indeed, for the great student of signs" (White, 34). By acknowledging the unknowableness of Japan, Barthes wants to expose our own Western need, especially evident in the travel genre, to find depth and to know. He offers plenty of comparisons between East and West—food, interior design, theater—but Tokyo itself provides a particularly telling example. Tokyo is a city with a center—the imperial palace—but the center is empty. It houses an emperor who is never seen, in a place where no one ever goes. Whether or not Tokyo shares this characteristic with other great cities does not concern Barthes. Almost smugly he reminds us that in Western metaphysics, "for which every center is the site of truth, the center of our cities is always *full*" (*Empire*, 30). According to Barthes, our dedication to truth, fullness, and depth is the foundation of the Western myth of wanting to know what foreign cultures are all about. Can we ever really unpack that and leave it behind any more than we can empty our city centers?

It all depends on what we're after. If, like Paul Bowles's travelers in *The Sheltering Sky* we demand authenticity or pureness in ourselves as well as in foreign cultures, we shall indeed "go crazy" (Clifford, 1). Or, if we insist with Barthes that the choice is one of either depth or surface but not both, then the world will indeed be inscrutable. James Clifford suggests another way that results from seeing cultures "not as organically unified or traditionally continuous but rather as negotiated, present processes" (Clifford, 273). The impurity of cultural exchange does not bother

Clifford as it did Bowles or even Lévi-Strauss. As Clifford says of our contemporary "creolized" world,

> Intervening in an interconnected world, one is always, to varying degrees, "inauthentic": caught between cultures, implicated in others. Because discourse in global power systems is elaborated vis-á-vis, a sense of difference or distinctness can never be located solely in the continuity of a culture or a tradition. Identity is conjunctural, not essential. (Clifford, 11)

Insisting on depth, permanence, and authenticity for our own world or for an alien one is to place ourselves squarely in the place of truth. Unfixing oneself so that place cannot equal truth is to adopt a more nomadic position. Writing as a displaced exile allows one to embark upon a "two-directional journey examining the realities of both sides of cultural differences so that they may mutually question each other, and thereby generate a realistic image of human possibilities and a self-confidence for the explorer grounded in comparative understanding rather than ethnocentrism."[5] The texts that result from this "two-directional journey" tend, as we have seen, to rely heavily on fantasy and evocation rather than on facts and representation since the appeal to science or truth is abandoned along with the concept of a static, finalized culture.

What these concerns to represent the other fairly, to admit even to the impossibility of gathering into one cohesive narrative any cultural experience outside our own, mean to the travel genre are uncertain. Perhaps it is finally the reader's task to treat travel books as culturally biased texts instead of documents of pure fact. As Foucault reminds us, "We must not imagine that the world turns toward us a legible face which we would only have to decipher. The world is not the accomplice of our knowledge."[6] Like the exotic museum objects in glass cases brought by travelers to the West from New Zealand and Nigeria, travel books can tell only part of the story. Like the Maori spear brought back as material object with a narrative to tell, the travel book is also a decontextualized object, forever disembodied from its source, collected and arranged with discursive constraints that are both personal and political. For travel writers, anthropologists, and museum curators, in order to displace oneself and collapse distance between self and other, the curiosity that is assumed at the beginning of this study on the part of both reader and writer must move beyond its infantile acceptance of things and stories for their shock value alone. If we are to understand those who are different from us, we must constantly negotiate the entangled space between us.

# Notes and References

Chapter 1

1. Herman Melville, *Moby-Dick* (1851; reprint, New York: W. W. Norton & Company, 1967), 56; hereafter cited in the text.

2. Joseph Campbell, *The Hero With a Thousand Faces* (Princeton: Princeton University Press, 1968), 3–25; hereafter cited in the text.

3. Janis P. Stout, *The Journey Narrative in American Literature: Patterns and Development* (Westport, Conn.: Greenwood Press, 1983), 14; hereafter cited in the text.

4. Paul Fussell, *The Norton Book of Travel* (New York: W. W. Norton, 1987), 21; hereafter cited in the text.

5. Herodotus, *The Histories*, ed. Walter Blanco and Jennifer Tolbert Blanco; trans. Walter Blanco (New York: Norton, 1992), 78; hereafter cited in the text.

6. Mary Campbell, *The Witness and the Other World: Exotic European Travel Writing, 400–1600* (Ithaca: Cornell University Press, 1988), 15–20; hereafter cited in the text.

7. John Wilkinson, ed., *Egeria's Travels to the Holy Land* (Jerusalem: Ariel, 1981), 111; hereafter cited in the text.

8. Marco Polo, *The Travels of Marco Polo,* trans. Teresa Waugh (London: Sidgwick and Jackson, 1984), 175; hereafter cited in the text.

9. See especially Frederick Turner, *Beyond Geography* (New York: Viking, 1980) and William Brandon, *New Worlds for Old* (Athens, Ohio: Ohio University Press, 1986).

10. Christopher Columbus, *The Voyage of Christopher Columbus*, trans. John Cummins (London: Weidenfeld & Nicholson, 1992), 97; hereafter cited in the text.

11. See note 8.

12. See especially Frederick Turner, *Beyond Geography* (New York: Viking, 1980), 173.

13. Sir Walter Ralegh, "The Discovery of Guiana," in *The Works of Sir Walter Raleigh, Kt.* (New York; Burt Franklin, 1829), 8:396; hereafter cited in the text.

14. William C. Spengemann, *The Adventurous Muse: The Poetics of American Fiction 1789–1900* (New Haven: Yale University Press, 1989), 38; hereafter cited in the text.

15. Johannes Fabian, *Time and the Other: How Anthropology Makes Its Object* (New York: Columbia University Press, 1983), 6; hereafter cited in the text.

16. Mary Louise Pratt, *Imperial Eyes: Travel Writing and Transculturation.* (London: Routledge, 1992), 15; hereafter cited in the text.

17. Lady Mary Wortley Montagu, *Turkish Embassy Letters* (1763; reprint, Athens: University of Georgia Press, 1993), 58; hereafter cited in the text.

18. Laurence Sterne, *A Sentimental Journey through France and Italy* (1768; reprint, ed. Graham Petrie, Baltimore: Penguin Books, 1967), 11; hereafter cited in the text.

19. Mungo Park, *Travels in the Interior Districts of Africa* (1799; reprint, London: J. M. Dent & Sons, 1930); hereafter cited in the text.

20. Dennis Porter, *Haunted Journeys: Desire and Transgression in European Travel Writing* (Princeton: Princeton University Press, 1991), 10–11; hereafter cited in the text.

21. Janet Varner Gunn, *Autobiography: Toward a Poetics of Experience* (Philadelphia: University of Pennsylvania Press, 1982), 60; hereafter cited in the text.

22. William Bartram, *The Travels of William Bartram* (1791; reprint, ed. Francis Harper, New Haven: Yale University Press, 1958), 312; hereafter cited in the text.

23. See Charles Norton Coe, *Wordsworth and the Literature of Travel* (New York: Octagon Books, 1979).

24. See William C. Spengemann, *The Adventurous Muse* (New Haven: Yale University Press, 1977) and Janis P. Stout, *The Journey Narrative in American Literature* (Westport: Greenwood Press, 1983).

25. Henry David Thoreau, *The Journal of Henry David Thoreau,* ed. Bradford Torrey and Francis H. Allen (Boston: Houghton Mifflin Company, 1906), 2:281; hereafter cited in the text.

26. Henry David Thoreau, *A Week on the Concord and Merrimack Rivers* (1849; reprint, Princeton: Princeton University Press, 1983), 12; hereafter cited in the text.

27. Charles Darwin, *The Voyage of the Beagle* (1839; reprint, New York: Bantam Books, 1972), 438; hereafter cited in the text.

28. Paul Fussell, *Abroad: British Literary Traveling between the Wars* (New York: Oxford University Press, 1980), 50–64; hereafter cited in the text.

29. Samuel Hynes, *The Auden Generation: Literature and Politics in England in the 1930s* (New York: Viking Press, 1977), 228; hereafter cited in the text.

30. Evelyn Waugh, *When the Going Was Good* (Boston: Little, Brown, 1984), 93; hereafter cited in the text.

31. Northrop Frye, *Anatomy of Criticism* (Princeton: Princeton University Press, 1957), 192; hereafter cited in the text.

32. Alan Wilde, *Horizons of Assent: Modernism, Postmodernism, and the Ironic Imagination* (Philadelphia: University of Pennsylvania Press, 1987), 10; hereafter cited in the text.

33. Dean Maccannell, *The Tourist: A New Theory of the Leisure Class* (New York: Schocken Books, 1976), 3; hereafter cited in the text.

34. Thomas Parkindon, ed., *A Casebook on the Beat* (New York: Thomas Y. Crowell, 1961), 213; hereafter cited in the text.

35. Claude Lévi-Strauss, *Tristes Tropiques* (1955; reprint, trans. John and Doreen Weightman, New York: Schocken Books, 1976), 38; hereafter cited in the text.

36. Paul Bowles, *Their Heads Are Green and Their Hands Are Blue* (New York: Ecco Press, 1984), 113; hereafter cited in the text.

37. Geoffrey O'Brian, "White Light White Heat," *Voice Literary Supplement* 14 (1986): 10; hereafter cited in the text.

38. Linda Hutcheon, *A Poetics of Postmodernism* (New York: Routledge, 1988), 115; hereafter cited in the text.

39. James Clifford, *The Predicament of Culture: Twentieth-Century Ethnography, Literature, and Art* (Cambridge: Harvard University Press, 1988), 173; hereafter cited in the text.

40. Jeremy Harding, "Polisario," *Granta* 26 (Spring 1989): 26; hereafter cited in the text.

## Chapter 2

1. Frank Brady, introduction to *Boswell on the Grand Tour: Italy, Corsica, and France* (New York: McGraw-Hill), ix; hereafter cited in the text.

2. James Boswell, *Boswell's London Journal, 1762–1763*, ed. Frederick A. Pottle (New York: McGraw-Hill, 1950), 49–50; cited in the text as *London*. Subsequent references to Boswell's journals: *Holland Journal*, ed. Frederick A. Pottle (New York: McGraw-Hill, 1953; cited as *Holland* in the text; *Boswell on the Grand Tour: Germany and Switzerland 1764*, ed. Frederick A. Pottle (New York: McGraw-Hill, 1953), cited as *G&S* in the text; *Boswell on the Grand Tour: Italy, Corsica, and France 1765–1766*, ed. Frank Brady and Frederick A. Pottle (New York: McGraw-Hill, 1955), cited as *ICF* in the text.

## Chapter 3

1. Gertrude Bell, *Syria: The Desert and the Sown* (1907; reprint, London: William Heinemann, 1919), 1; hereafter cited in the text.

2. The prevailing notion that the phenomenon of women traveling alone in the mid–nineteenth century was an anomaly is

beginning to be disputed. See, for instance, Shirley Foster *Across New Worlds* (New York: Harrester, 1990) and Sara Mills *Discourses of Difference* (London: Routledge, 1991) for discussions on the "many hundreds" of Victorian women travelers and their reasons for going.

3. It is perhaps our own modern cultural baggage that demands we conflate radical lives with radical politics. For reasons owing more to their upbringing than to their desire for travel, women like Mary Kingsley were defenders, at home, of the status quo. See the many books on Victorian women travelers in the biblographic essay that follows for further reference.

4. Mary H. Kingsley, *Travels in West Africa* (1897; reprint, Boston: Beacon Press, 1988), 659; hereafter cited in the text as *Africa*.

5. Sara Mills, *Discourses of Difference: An Analysis of Women's Travel Writing and Colonialism* (London: Routledge, 1993); hereafter cited in the text.

6. Dea Birkett, *Spinsters Abroad: Victorian Lady Explorers* (Oxford: Basil Blackwell, 1989); hereafter cited in the text.

7. Sandra M. Gilbert and Susan Gubar, *The Madwoman in the Attic: The Woman Writer and the Nineteenth-Century Literary Imagination* (New Haven: Yale University Press, 1979); hereafter cited in the text.

8. Elspeth Huxley, introduction to *Travels in West Africa*, abridged ed. (London: J. M. Dent & Sons, 1987), 3–4; hereafter cited in the text.

9. For an analysis of this kind of "creolization" between cultures, see James Clifford, *The Predicament of Culture: Twentieth-Century Ethnography, Literature, and Art* (Cambridge: Harvard University Press, 1988) and Mary Louise Pratt, *Imperial Eyes: Travel Writing and Transculturation* (London: Routledge, 1992).

## Chapter 4

1. T. S. Eliot, "Little Gidding," in *T. S. Eliot: The Complete Poems and Plays* (New York: Harcourt, Brace & World, 1952).

2. Graham Greene, *Collected Essays* (London: Penguin, 1988), 17; hereafter cited in the text as *Essays*.

3. Graham Greene, *Journey without Maps* (1936; reprint, London: Heinemann & Bodley Head, 1978), ix; hereafter cited in the text as *Maps*.

4. For a more thorough understanding of Greene's childhood, see Norman Sherry, *The Life of Graham Greene, Vol. I: 1904–1939* (New York: Viking Penguin, 1989).

Chapter 5

1. Peter Matthiessen, *The Snow Leopard* (New York: Viking Penguin, 1978), 11; hereafter cited in the text as *Snow*.

Chapter 6

1. J. J. Healy, "Friction, Voice, and the Rough Ground of Feeling: V. S. Naipaul after Twenty-Five Years," *University of Toronto Quarterly* 55 (Fall 1985): 58; hereafter cited in the text.

2. V. S. Naipaul, *The Mimic Men* (New York: Penguin Books, 1967).

3. V. S. Naipaul, *An Area of Darkness* (1964; reprint, New York: Vintage Books, 1981), 45; hereafter cited in the text as *Area*.

4. Robert K. Morris, *Paradoxes of Order* (Columbia: University of Missouri Press, 1975), 75; hereafter cited in the text.

Chapter 7

1. James Clifford, *The Predicament of Culture: Twentieth-Century Ethnography, Literature, and Art* (Cambridge: Harvard University Press, 1988), 14; hereafter cited in the text.

2. Bruce Chatwin, *The Songlines* (New York: Viking, 1987), 18; hereafter cited in the text as *Songlines*.

3. Bruce Chatwin, *In Patagonia* (New York: Penguin Books, 1988), 1; hereafter cited in the text as *Patagonia*.

4. Paul Theroux, Interview by George Plimpton, The Poetry Center. New York, December 18, 1989.

5. Bruce Chatwin, "The Songlines Quartet," *New York Review of Books* 21–22 (January 1989): 50; hereafter cited in the text as "Quartet."

6. Ian Buruma, "The Wanderlust of Bruce Chatwin," *Traveler* (March 1989): 94; hereafter cited in the text.

7. Diane Ackerman, "Home Was Where the Road Was," *New York Times Book Review* (September 10, 1989): 9; hereafter cited in the text.

8. David Plante, "Tales of Chatwin," *Esquire* (October 1990): 183–90; hereafter cited in the text.

Chapter 8

1. Mary Louise Pratt, "Scratches on the Face of the Country; or, What Mr. Barrow Saw in the Land of the Bushmen," In *"Race," Writing, and Difference,* ed. Henry Louis Gates Jr. (Chicago: University of Chicago Press, 1986), 139–40; hereafter cited in the text.

2. Paul Theroux, *The Old Patagonian Express: By Train through the Americas* (1979; reprint, New York: Pocket Books, 1980), 364; hereafter cited in the text as *Express.*

3. Roland Barthes, *Empire of Signs* (1970; reprint, trans. Richard Howard, New York: Farrar, Strauss, and Giroux, 1982); hereafter cited in the text as *Empire.*

4. Edmund White, "From Albert Camus to Roland Barthes," *New York Times Book Review* (September 12, 1982): 1–34; hereafter cited in the text.

5. Michael M. J. Fischer, "Ethnicity and the Arts of Memory," in *Writing Culture: The Poetics and Politics of Ethnography,* ed. James Clifford and George E. Marcus (Berkeley: University of California Press, 1986), 21; hereafter cited in the text.

6. Michel Foucault, "The Order of Discourse," in *Untying the Text: A Post-Structural Reader,* ed. R. Young (London: Routledge & Regan Paul, 1981), 48–79; hereafter cited in the text.

# Bibliographic Essay

The critical response to the literature of travel falls naturally into three types of analyses: historical overview; influence on other genres; and travel book as cultural study. Most critics have been reluctant to give special attention to the travel writing of major authors, most of whom write fiction and other forms as well. Critical analyses of the travel writing of the major practitioners of this study can normally be found in standard critical works on each author or, in the case of Mary Kingsley, in the vast amount of material on women Victorian travel writers.

## Historical Overview

By far the best in-depth overview of the earliest travel writing is *The Witness and the Other World: Exotic European Travel Writing, 400–1600* (Ithaca: Cornell University Press, 1988) by Mary B. Campbell. In scope it is restricted to premodern European accounts of travel to Asia, the most alien place for Europeans of that time. For Campbell these accounts are examples of "a history of the slow assembling of the features that now identify a work as 'travel literature' "(Campbell, 5). Beginning with the fifth-century nun Egeria and ending with Sir Walter Ralegh, Campbell focuses on how these works "grapple with literary problems of presentation—self-presentation as well as presentation of the other and the external world—with an immediacy unmatched in other medieval prose genres"(Campbell, 6). In her introduction she spends some time with the question of genre.

> This is a genre composed of other genres, as well as one that importantly contributed to the genesis of the modern novel and the renaissance of autobiography. It is a genre that confronts, at their extreme limit, representational tasks proper to a number of literary kinds: the translation of experience into narrative and description, of the strange into the visible, of observation into the verbal construct of fact; the deployment of personal voice in the service of transmitting information (or of creating devotional texts); the manipulation of rhetorical figures for ends other than ornament. Some of these demands are familiar to the "participant observers" of ethnography, others to writers and critics of fictional realism or historiography. All of them are important to the analysis of travel writing. (Campbell, 6)

Campbell is most interested in the experience of the self—the "witness"—translating the experience of the other world into narrative. For that reason she begins her study with Egeria. Unlike Herodotus and other earlier travel writers for whom travel was a way to accumulate data, Campbell believes that because Egeria's religious quest to the holy land is a personal one, self "becomes necessary as a rhetorical presence" (Campbell, 15).

This idea of self, which is so central to the modern travel book, is Campbell's chief concern. She traces, among other things, the development of the importance of the witness to travel narratives. From Egeria to Marco Polo to Mandeville and finally to Ralegh, Campbell guides us steadily toward a more recognizable rendering of experience through self.

Most guides to the older travel narratives are not as philosophically oriented as Campbell. Boies Penrose's classic study on Renaissance travel, *Travel and Discovery in the Renaissance, 1420–1620* (Cambridge: Harvard University Press, 1955), although an admirable and necessary treatment of the importance of travel and discovery in the Renaissance, devotes only one chapter to the literature that resulted from those journeys. Yet this worthy compression of the thousands of travelogues and ship's logs published by, among others, the Hakluyt Society is invaluable to the student of the travel narrative. Penrose chooses the best of the Renaissance travelogues and dispenses with the minor figures. It is further helpful that he divides the chapters geographically: "The Literature of the Portuguese Discoveries and Conquests," "The Literature of Spanish Overseas Enterprise," "The Geographical Literature of the Remainder of Continental Europe," and "Tudor Geographical Literature."

A more purely literary study that begins where Penrose ends is Wayne Franklin's dense book *Discoverers, Explorers, Settlers: Diligent Writers of Early America* (Chicago: The University of Chicago Press, 1979). Franklin's complex argument is that there is initially a problematic relationship between word and event, especially for the writer of a travel narrative. The writings of Columbus and Cortés are full of misapprehensions and doubtful descriptions that, as Franklin says, are a direct result of the explorers not having appropriate language for their very new experiences. "Indeed, the recognition that his language was inadequate to what he perceived was itself an event, a consequence of his voyage which became a kind of 'static' in his medium—and hence a sign of his general position in America" (Franklin, 4). Because of the difficulty of adapting European words to American experience, there developed, according to Franklin, a kind of myth of America in travel writing that persisted throughout early American writing itself, and perhaps even established itself firmly in the American psyche as well. This myth "would indicate that Old World words indeed could control American events, that art could organize a multitude of unseen . . . circumstances" (Franklin, 5). In this way Franklin sees that the types of early American travel writing (discovering, exploring, and settling) all tangled with this same myth. So that ultimately, even the American pioneer himself adopts this myth and, going west, turns into a kind of sainted hero as he pushes back the unknown.

Despite the importance of these early travel accounts and their undeniable influence on later travel narratives, the eighteenth century really marks the beginning of the travel book as we know it today. Not surprisingly, much critical energy has been spent on that period's writing and its practitioners. For its full treatment of the history of travel in the eighteenth century, William Edward Mead's *The Grand Tour in the Eighteenth Century* (New York: Benjamin Blom, 1914) provides essential background to the phenomenon of the explosion of travel in that century. Any study of the eighteenth-century travel book would not be complete without Percy G. Adams's *Travelers and Travel Liars: 1660–1800* (Berkeley: University of California Press, 1962). As Adams says,

> "This book deals . . . with authentic travel accounts that in an Age of Reason told untruths, with pseudo voyages that were designed to make the public believe they were real, with charges and counter-charges of lying, with the reasons that brought these falsehoods, these travels, and these charges into existence, with the devices that writers of travel books used in fooling or attempting to fool readers, and with the amazing results that these devices achieved." (Adams *Liars*, vii)

Aside from its sheer quirkiness, Percy's book is a good indicator of the popularity of both travel and travel writing in the eighteenth century.

Because of the large number of travel books it was inevitable that at some point genre classifications had to be considered by critics, and it is appropriate that they concern the eighteenth century. It is somewhat surprising that there are so few attempts at a definition of genre for the travel book. Charles Batten's sane effort in *Pleasurable Instruction: Form and Convention in Eighteenth-Century Travel Literature* (Berkeley: University of California Press, 1978) is an admirable beginning. Batten warns the reader that we ought not to apply the same standards to the eighteenth-century travel book as we do to the modern. For instance our predilection for more autobiographical works would not have suited the eighteenth-century audience. However, as we have seen in this study, all the elements of the travel book were available to the eighteenth-century travel writer. But, as Batten argues, the goal for writers of the latter part of the century was to get those elements in balance. The two most important elements were narrative and description, one tending toward the autobiographical, the other toward the scientific. In this way the eighteenth-century travel book could both please with its more intimate narrative and instruct with its scientific data. For Batten it is the "golden mean" which aims neither for pure autobiography nor pure description that characterizes the beginnings of the modern travel book in the eighteenth century. But by the end of the century, as Batten notes, travel descriptions begin to "derive from the imagination of the traveler, reflecting how he personally felt in foreign settings"(Batten, 119). Batten's book is important because it attempts to make the distinctions that aim toward a definition of the genre.

The personal element, so prominent in the modern travel book, is the subject of Dennis Porter's study of a surprisingly wide range of travel narratives from Boswell to Barthes in *Haunted Journeys: Desire and Transgression in European Travel Writing* (Princeton: Princeton University Press, 1991). Using the twin themes of desire and transgression, Porter views travel and travel writing as a kind of Freudian activity. In his studies of Boswell, Diderot, Bouganville, Cook, Stendhal, Darwin, Flaubert, Freud, D. H. Lawrence, T. E. Lawrence, Gide, Lévi-Strauss, Barthes, and Naipaul, Porter shows that these "writing travelers put their fantasies on display often in spite of themselves. In one way or another, they are always writing about lives they want or do not want to live, the lost objects of their desire or the phobias that threaten to disable them" (Porter, 13). Despite this seemingly limited focus, Porter's book manages to touch on many important critical issues: the problems of representation, the Foucaultian nexus of power and knowledge, and the Bakhtinian notion of the creation of the self through a dialogic encounter with the other. Porter's book, though seemingly broad, contains some of the best studies of individual travel writers.

An increasingly popular topic for critical study is the woman traveler. *The Blessings of a Good Thick Skirt* (London: Collins, 1986) by Mary Russell is a good introduction to the phenomenon of women travelers from Egeria to Earhart and attempts to answer the question of purpose. "This book," says Russell "is less concerned with theories than with the reasons offered by women themselves as to why they soar off into the dawn skies" (Russell, 15). Most of the books devoted to women travelers tend to have this tone. In effect, their authors treat their subjects as eccentrics and wonder at their bravery. Unfortunately these types of works add little to any consideration of genre. Perhaps because of their persistent oddity, Victorian women travelers seem to acquire more attention than any other group. *Victorian Lady Travellers* (London: Routledge, 1965) by Dorothy Middleton offers a biographical survey of seven women travelers: Isabella Bird, Marianne North, Fanny Bullock Workman, May French Sheldon, Annie Taylor, Kate Marsden, and Mary Kingsley. The book is short and offers little beyond the facts of their lives and their journeys—many of them quite remarkable. *Spinsters Abroad: Victorian Lady Explorers* (Oxford: Basil Blackwell, 1989) by Dea Birkett, a later book, studies these Victorian women travelers in a thematic way, grouping them around the experiences of departure, adventure, and return, rather than by individual author. Birkett attempts to account not only for what these women did but also why they did it and what, if any, their particular female perspectives might have to offer. *Across New Worlds* (New York: Harrester, 1990) by Shirley Foster is similarly organized, but offers specific evidence for the book's thesis that, despite the difficulty of generalizing, some common elements do seem to appear in women's travel accounts. Foster argues that these are the thrill and enthusiasm with which women write about their travels, inspired perhaps by the sense of escape; the sexual and libidinous aspect of this escape from the norms, giving the texts a subconscious sexual voice; focus on the family and on women; and, finally, undeniable sympathy with the other. Two other books that treat nineteenth-century women travel writers in an adequate, introductory way: *Victorian Women Travel Writers in Africa* (Boston: Twayne, 1982) by Catherine Barnes Stevenson and *Travelling Ladies* (London: Jupiter, 1980) by Alexandra Allen.

An excellent book by Sara Mills attempts a deeper analysis of women's roles in the production of travel narratives than any of the preceding studies and is a welcome addition to the criticism of travel writing as a whole. *Discourses of Difference: An Analysis of Women's Travel Writing* (London: Routledge, 1993) offers an analysis of British women travel writers during the mid nineteenth to early twentieth century who journeyed to colonized countries. Mills is especially concerned with how women writers of this period might be read as part of the ongoing colonial discourse and the extent of their contribution. To this end Mills sees that women's travel writing of this period was both received and written differently than the male texts of the same era. Because of these differences, writers such as Mary Kingsley in particular had difficulty assuming the "imperial voice" of her male counterparts. In order to expand her discourse to include contemporary critical theory, Mills takes as her philosophical framework a blend of Foucault and feminism, particularly where the two verge on the subject of power systems, and by doing so, invites us to understand women's travel writing not from the standpoint of the authors' femininity or eccentricities, but rather as part of the discourse about feminism, colonialism, and the travel genre. There are several anthologies of essays about travel writing that cover a wide range of material and ideas. The May 1992 edition of *Prose Studies* (London: Frank Cass & Co.) is devoted entirely to "The Art of Travel." In it are nine essays about travel writing, ranging in time and interest from Columbus to Evelyn Waugh. A feminist research collective from Washington State University has amassed the results of their studies about the female travel experience into a book called *Women and the Journey* (Pullman: Washington State University Press, 1993). Although the book also treats the female journey in fiction, the essays about travel narratives, especially those by slave women, are particularly interesting. The modern travel narrative is given critical attention in Michael Kowalewski's *Temperamental Journeys: Essays on the Modern Literature of Travel* (Athens: University of Georgia Press, 1992). Topics include postwar British travel writing, travel writers of the Great Plains, the guidebook industry, and women travelers. Individual modern writers such as Joan Didion, Paul Theroux, John McPhee, and Jonathan Raban are treated in individual essays. Reprinted here are some well-known essays about travel, including Michel Butor's "Travel and Writing" and a chapter from Paul Fussell's *Abroad*. What is perhaps most helpful about this book is the bibliography of travel writing since 1900, arranged by author's nationality. Here one finds works (albeit few) by travel writers from Togoland, Egypt, and Nigeria. This inclusion of non-Western writers is especially important since most critical studies (including this one) are heavily weighted toward the Anglo-American writer.

## Influence Studies

A rich source of material on the literature of travel has been those studies that seek to trace the influence of travel accounts on other types of literature, particularly the novel. The relationship between the early explorers' accounts of their journeys forms the subject of Robert Ralston Cawley's book *Unpathed Waters: Studies in the Influence of the Voyagers on Elizabethan Literature* (New York: Octagon Books, 1967). Cawley not only considers the importance of Renaissance travelogues on such figures as Greene, Dekker, and Shakespeare but also spends much of his study accounting for the heritage that travelogues from the Middle Ages offered to these same writers. In a chapter called "The Spirit of the Voyagers" Cawley captures the compelling energy and power of the Renaissance traveler that allowed him to become such a great source of inspiration to sixteenth-century dramatists. A study that treats the travel book more directly is Percy G. Adams's *Travel Literature and the Evolution of the Novel* (Lexington: University Press of Kentucky, 1983). Adams examines the close contact between the travel account and the early novel and in doing so comes as close as any critic does in attempting a definition of the genre. His second chapter, "Travel Literature before 1800—Its History, Its Types, Its Influence," is valuable for its compression of a vast amount of historical information. Adams's central argument is that the travel account and the early novel shared many of the same concerns, primarily treading the same fine line between truth and artifice, between realist description and exotic fantasies. Structurally both travel account and novel depend on the quest motif. This basic, ageless structure also provides the genres some common elements such as a narrator and the action and characters he or she meets along the way. Adams's argument is convincing, and his book is particularly valuable because of its author's deep understanding of the travel genre as revealed in the richness of reference and example.

A classic influence study that Adams admires is one that traces the relationship between early travel accounts and two of Coleridge's poems, "The Rime of the Ancient Mariner" and "Kubla Khan." It is a lengthy book, nearly as mysterious as the poems themselves. *Road to Xanadu* (Boston: Houghton Mifflin Company, 1927) by John Livingston Lowes is a detective story told by a man who loves the scent of the hunt. Lowes tracks down everything Coleridge ever read, cross-referencing material until he sees a complex pattern of influence, particularly of travel accounts, on the imagination of the poet. It is a vast compendium of travelers' strange tales and as such gives a good indication of the wealth of exotic material contained in travelers' accounts as well as a fascinating study of the mind of the poet. A more straightforward account of that same kind of connection is to be found in William C. Spengemann's *The Adventurous Muse* (New Haven: Yale University Press, 1989). He describes his book's purpose quite clearly.

> Its subject is the emergence of the American Romantic novel out of two very different fictional poetics: a poetics of adventure, invented by the American travel writers to portray the metamorphosing world that appears to someone who stands on its moving frontier; and a poetics of domesticity, devised by certain highly influential English novelists to restrain and discredit this potentially subversive vision of reality. (Spengemann, 3)

It is this "subversive" material that most interests Spengemann since, for him, it gives American literature its peculiar power. His book, along with those by Cawley, Adams, and Lowes, are important secondary reading because they offer strong support for the enduring vitality and importance of the genre.

## Cultural Studies

Several very exciting studies by anthropologists and literary critics alike have centered on the way in which travel writing, like its scientific double, ethnography, tends to be Eurocentric and even imperialistic. Some interesting things happen when these claims are made. One is that travel writing can be seen as ethnographic discourse and is, therefore, complicit in the movement to colonize the world by Europe and America. Following Foucault's conflation of knowledge with power, travel writing, certainly much of the older texts, can be regarded as "hegemonic discourse." James Clifford in his book *The Predicament of Culture* (Cambridge: Harvard University Press, 1988) treats travel writing and museum collecting as efforts to both know and hold sway over the other. Who, Clifford asks, has the authority to describe in narrative or display by way of artifacts another group of people with the intent of knowing the identity and authenticity of that group? Travel writing comes under close scrutiny in a chapter called "Tell about Your Trip," in which Clifford analyzes the travel journal of Michel Leiris, *L'Afrique fantôme*. What interests Clifford is how Leiris is caught between wanting to write a travel narrative that purports to understand and reveal the African, and the impossibility of such an undertaking. "Interrupting the smooth ethnographic story of an access to Africa, *[L'Afrique fantôme]* undermines the assumption that self and other can be gathered in a stable narrative coherence" (Clifford, 173).

When one accepts the difficulty of any text about the other—travel, artistic, or ethnographic—having authority to describe or to know that other, another interesting thing happens. Ethnographic texts also become a source of literary criticism. Instead of treating ethnographic reports as purely scientific data, gathered by purely objective field workers, anthropologist Clifford Geertz reads texts by Lévi-Strauss, Malinowski, and Mead in much the same way we would read a travel book or even a novel, with an eye to author, style, and purpose. In his *Works and Lives: The Anthropologist as Author* (Stanford: Stanford University Press, 1988), Geertz makes his case for this kind of study.

> The illusion that ethnography is a matter of sorting strange and irregular facts into familiar and orderly categories—this is magic, that is technology—has long since been exploded. What it is instead, however, is less clear. (Geertz, 1)

What "it" becomes for Geertz is an opportunity for looking at some classic works of anthropology in a new light to show how their authors build texts that in turn build a world readers are asked to believe in.

This famous blurring of genres that seek to represent the other does not surprise Mary Louise Pratt who sees a rich history in the personal-narrative-as-scientific-document. In "Field Work in Common Places," one of the essays in the excellent book *Writing Culture: The Poetics and Politics of Ethnography* (Berkeley: University of California Press, 1986), Pratt maintains that

> [t]he practice of combining personal narrative and objectified description is hardly the invention of modern ethnography.... By the early sixteenth century in Europe, it was conventional for travel accounts to consist of a combination of first-person narration, recounting one's trip, and description of flora and fauna or regions passed through. (Pratt 1986, 33)

She goes on to explore this close connection between what the travel narrative does quite explicitly and what the ethnographic account does in spite of itself. As Geertz does, Pratt cites example after example of ethnographers relating feelings, exposing themselves as observing selves as most travel writers do quite readily. And, she concludes, if ethnologists would own up to what they are doing, "[t]hen it becomes possible . . . to liberate oneself from [tropes], not by doing away with tropes (which is not possible) but by appropriating and inventing new ones (which is)" (Pratt 1986, 50). These observations lead back to the question of authority in travel writing and ethnography, and the fictionalizing of data, a particularly rich vein in cultural studies. With anthropologists, literary critics, students of culture, and "difference" all convening on the travel accounts, we are forced to see the older accounts in a new light. Several of the contributors to "Race," Writing, and Difference (Chicago: The University of Chicago Press, 1985), edited by Henry Louis Gates Jr., use the texts of travel writers to show how the idea of difference and race are instituted in narratives about the other.

Mary Louise Pratt extends her ideas about travel writing and imperialism in an excellent full-length study called Imperial Eyes: Travel Writing and Transculturation (London: Routledge, 1992). Pratt is not solely interested in pointing fingers at earlier writers, fixing and othering as they traveled. Instead she is intrigued by what she calls "the contact zone," that place where two cultures meet and share, albeit unequally, cultural material.

> The term "transculturation" in the title sums up my efforts in this direction. Ethnographers have used this term to describe how subordinated or marginalized groups select and invent from materials transmitted to them by a dominant metropolitan culture. (Pratt 1992, 6)

Pratt is interested in a more intriguing sharing of material.

> How have Europe's constructions of subordinated others been shaped by those others, by the constructions of themselves and their habitats that they presented to the Europeans? (Pratt 1992, 6)

As Pratt says, the "imperial metropolis" is always blind to this side of the transaction, due to Europe's "obsessive need to present and re-present its peripheries and its others continually to itself. Travel writing . . . is heavily organized in the service of that imperative" (Pratt 1992, 6).

One striking example of that imperative that Pratt offers is the "discovery" narrative of Sir Richard Burton, *Lake Regions of Central Africa*. Burton renders his "discovery" of Lake Tanganyika quite dramatically in his travel book. But, as Pratt reminds us, these discoveries in fact

> involved making one's way to the region and asking the local inhabitants if they knew of any big lakes, etc. in the area, then hiring them to take you there, whereupon with their guidance and support, you proceeded to discover what they already knew. (Pratt 1992, 202)

But, of course, for the preservation of the European sense of power and authority, it is important for Burton and most other early travel writers to claim discovery for themselves. Pratt contrasts this monarch-of-all-I-survey approach to Mary Kingsley's more self-effacing travel accounts where she is more often the butt of the joke rather than conquering hero. Instead of standing on a promontory claiming discovery of a local lake, Kingsley fends off crocodiles in her beloved swamps. Pratt's book has many concerns, but in the end it is a valuable but frankly ideological look at the genre. Pratt makes no apologies. "I described this book . . . as a study in genre as well as a critique of ideology. Scholarship on travel and exploration literature, such as it exists, has tended to develop along neither of these lines" (Pratt 1992, 10). As this survey of secondary readings on the subject of travel literature has suggested, Mary Louise Pratt is right. Scholarship is not extensive, and only recently has attention turned to the wider cultural issues implicit in the very act of travel writing.

# Recommended Titles

The following list of classic travel books is by no means exhaustive or complete. It is meant to be a starting place for readers unfamiliar with the range and diversity of travel literature, a place from which new discoveries can always be made.

Addison, Joseph. *Remarks on Several Parts of Italy*. 1705. Reprint, London: Bell & Son, 1914. A classic eighteenth-century travel book, but slow reading because of Addison's tendency to value erudition over anecdote.

Agee, James, and Walker Evans. *Let Us Now Praise Famous Men*. Boston: Houghton Mifflin, 1941. The now famous collaboration between writer and photographer about southern tenant farmers in 1936. Agee's contribution is a poetic testament to the struggles and the dignity of the working poor.

Auden, W.H., and Christopher Isherwood. *Journey to a War*. London: Faber & Faber, 1937. The authors spent six months in 1938 covering the Sino-Japanese war and produced a classic among travel books, some of which is written in verse by Auden. While in China the two meet the usual suspects of travel and writing, Peter Fleming and Robert Capa, and a host of Chinese officials and civilians who were also trying to make sense out of the war.

Barthes, Roland. *Empire of Signs*. 1970. Reprint, translated by Richard Howard. New York: Farrar, Strauss, and Giroux, 1982. Barthes turns his semiotician's eye on the "signs" of Japanese culture in a most unusual (un)travel book.

Bartram, William. *The Travels of William Bartram*. 1791. Reprint, edited by Francis Harper. New Haven: Yale University Press, 1958. A favorite of the Romantic poets for its exoticizing of the American southern landscape and its denizens.

Basho. *The Narrow Road to the Far North.* 1966. Reprint, translated by Dorothy Britton. New York: Kodansha, 1974. Part journal of a trip to Northern Japan, part haiku series, Basho's travel narrative exhibits sensitivity to the beauty of his surroundings.

Bell, Gertrude. *Syria: The Desert and the Sown.* London: William Heinemann, 1907. An intrepid desert traveler and diplomat, Bell tells of an often perilous trip via horseback through the Middle East.

Bird, Isabella. *Journeys in Persia and Kurdistan.* 1891. Reprint, London: Virago Press, 1988. Bird travels to remote parts of the East and the American West. In this two volume work, she meticulously tells of economic, sociological, and religious ways of life. Often detail overshadows anecdote.

Bird, Isabella. *The Yangtze Valley and Beyond.* 1899. Reprint, Boston: Beacon Press, 1985. Bird's last great adventure, undertaken when she was 64, includes an exploration of the Yangtze river, a visit to the sparsely populated area of northwest China, and a snowy stay in the high Tibetan border region. Like all her travel books, this one is lengthy and detailed.

Boswell, James. *Boswell's Journal of a Tour to the Hebrides with Samuel Johnson, LL. D., 1773.* Edited by F. A. Pottle and C. H. Bennett. New York: Viking Press, 1936. A gossipy record of Boswell and Johnson's walking tour through Scotland, with much talking between the travelers and local wits.

Boswell, James. *Boswell on the Grand Tour: Germany and Switzerland and Germany, 1764.* Edited by F. A. Pottle. New York: McGraw-Hill, 1953. A highly personal and quirky account of a young man's Grand Tour of the continent.

Boswell, James. *Boswell on the Grand Tour: Italy, Corsica and France, 1765–1766.* Edited by Frank Brady and F. A. Pottle. New York: McGraw-Hill, 1955. Perhaps the best of Boswell's Grand Tour journals—sex in Italy, politics in Corsica.

Bowles, Paul. *Their Heads Are Green and Their Hands Are Blue.* New York: Random House, 1963. Sparse as the Moroccan landscape, these vignettes of North African life exhibit Bowles's contribution to "degree zero" tourism.

Burton, Sir Richard. *Personal Narrative of a Pilgrimage to El-Medinah and Mecca.* 1855. Reprint, New York: Dover, 1964. One of the legendary early explorers and travel writers, Burton describes his trip to Mecca disguised as an Arab in this two-volume book.

Byron, Robert. *The Road to Oxiana.* London: Macmillan, 1937. In this often overlooked masterpiece of the genre, we find Byron on an extremely literate and witty quest for non-Western architecture in the remote deserts of Iraq, Afghanistan, and Persia.

Columbus, Christopher. *The "Diario" of Christopher Columbus' First Voyage to America 1492–1493.* Abstracted by Fray Bartolomé de las Casas. Transcribed and translated into English, with notes and a concordance of the Spanish by Oliver Dunn and James E. Kelley Jr. Norman, Oklahoma: University of Oklahoma Press, 1989. The original diaries having long been lost, Las Casas's partly summarized, partly quoted 1530 version of Columbus's voyage to America is all we have. Parts of this first voyage are quoted and seem more immediate than the summaries. This edition is especially good.

Chatwin, Bruce and Paul Theroux. *Patagonia Revisited.* Boston: Houghton Mifflin, 1986. These two masters of the travel book share, in a very small volume, their personal responses to Patagonia. Much is repetition from each of their longer works on the subject.

Chatwin, Bruce. *In Patagonia.* New York: Summit, 1977. Chatwin's idiosyncratic style of collage and conversation is at its best here as he walks the length of Patagonia collecting stories of exiles and outlaws.

Chatwin, Bruce. *The Songlines.* New York: Viking, 1987. An odd travel book, it combines Chatwin's "Notes" on a larger work on nomadism with the story of the Aboriginal Songlines.

Clemens, Samuel. (Mark Twain). *Innocents Abroad.* 1869. Reprint, New York: Heritage Press, 1962. The not-so-innocent Twain mixed up with a boatload of American religious tourists makes for great reading especially when Twain and his group try to outwit the European hustlers.

Cooper, James Fenimore. *Gleanings in Europe.* 1837. Reprint, Albany: State University of New York Press, 1980. Written in epistolary style and generally concerned with social and political issues, a volume each is devoted to France, England, and Italy. Cooper is often critical of Europeans, but in the volume on France he tells of his meeting with the aging Sir Walter Scott.

Dana, Richard Henry. *Two Years before the Mast.* New York: Harper Bros., 1840. In the travel-adventure mode, Dana records his time spent on a merchant ship—immensely popular reading in the mid–nineteenth century.

Darwin, Charles. *The Voyage of the Beagle.* 1839. Reprint, New York: P. F. Collier, 1965. Full of the naturalist's data on South America and the Pacific, but surprisingly personal as well.

David-Neel, Alexandra. *My Journey to Lhasa: The Personal Story of the Only White Woman who Succeeded in Entering the Forbidden City.* London: William Heinemann, 1927. The title suggests only part of this amazing story of a French woman's nearly suicidal trip to Tibet.

Defoe, Daniel. *A Tour thro' the Whole Islands of Great Britain.* 1724–1726. Reprint, abridged and edited by P. N. Furbanks and W. R. Owens, New Haven: Yale University Press, 1991. One of the best early British travel books, this is a lengthy one: three volumes on England, Scotland, and Ireland. The British volume provides an especially good look at the progress and plenty of Britain in the 1720s. This edition is especially useful for its contemporary maps and paintings.

Dickens, Charles. *American Notes and Pictures from Italy*. London: Oxford University Press, 1974. This edition combines two of Dickens travel pieces, originally published separately. *Notes* (1842) takes us to various and unusual "tourist" stops: a poor house, a prison, an asylum for the insane. In *Pictures* (1846) Dickens evolves from social critic to art critic.

Didion, Joan. *Miami*. New York: Simon & Schuster, 1987. Didion's work is a good example of the success of the mixture of investigative journalism and travel writing. This book is especially valuable for her work on the Cuban-American community in Miami.

Didion, Joan. *Salvador*. New York: Simon & Schuster, 1983. Like *Miami*, this book tells as much about politics as it does about place.

Durrell, Lawrence. *Prospero's Cell: A Guide to the Landscape and Manners of Corcyra*. London: Faber & Faber, 1945. One of Durrell's best travel books, he writes about his beloved Corfu—its history and people, but mostly its spirit.

Egeria. *Egeria's Travels*. Translated by John Wilkinson. Jerusalem: Ariel, 1981. Written originally as letters home in the fifth century (C.E.), this is probably the first travel book to have a narrator who is conscious of her role as a guide to foreign places.

Emerson, Ralph Waldo. *English Traits*. 1856. Reprint, edited by Howard Mumford Jones, Cambridge: Harvard University Press, 1966. A valuable book about mid-nineteenth-century England by a foremost American philosopher. Essentially sympathetic to Britain, this account is not in the personal-travel-account mode. Instead Emerson travels as a sociologist and historian and shows a great mind at work on a foreign culture.

Fenton, James. *All the Wrong Places: Adrift in the Politics of the Pacific Rim*. New York: Atlantic Monthly Press, 1988. A good example of post-tourism dark humor as well as political-travel writing. The section on the Philippines is especially good.

Fermor, Patrick Leigh. *Mani: Travels in the Southern Peloponnese*. London: John Murray, 1958. A learned and curious travel writer of the 1950s, Fermor's book on Greece is really more anthropological, focusing on the history and people of the remote region of Mani.

Fleming, Peter. *Brazilian Adventure*. London: Jonathan Cape, 1933. One of the major travel writers between the wars, Fleming's books were very popular. This book is more humorous than most of Fleming's others, comparable in its ironic tone to Twain's *Innocents Abroad*.

Fuller, Margaret. *At Home and Abroad or Things and Thoughts in America and Europe*. Edited by A. B. Fuller. Boston: Crosby, Nichols, & Co.,

1856. A member of Emerson's inner circle, Fuller married an Italian marquis and lived in Italy for sometime, befriending, among others, the Brownings. Her unique, liberal perspective on Rome during the Italian Revolution is particularly noteworthy here. The manuscript for this book was recovered from the wreck of the *Elizabeth* near Fire Island, N.Y., where it sank drowning Fuller, her husband, and daughter.

Gide, André. *Travels in the Congo.* 1927. Reprint, translated by Dorothy Bussy, New York: Knopf, 1929. A day-by-day account of Gide's nine-month trip to central Africa; it is beautifully written and perceptive without being romantic.

Greene, Graham. *Journey without Maps.* 1936. Reprint, London: William Heinemann, 1978. One of the best books of the between-the-wars travel genre, Greene takes us into his psyche as well as into the heart of Liberia and Sierra Leone on this often frantic four-week march.

Greene, Graham. *The Lawless Roads.* 1939. Reprint, London: Penguin, 1982. The source for his novel, *The Power and the Glory*, this book details Greene's trip to Mexico in the late 1930s to discover the effects of the anticlerical purges of President Calles.

Herodotus. *The History of Herodotus.* Translated by Canon Rawlinson. London: Murray, 1897. The "father of history" tells of his fifth-century (B.C.E.) travels around the Mediterranean, gathering information about the Persian wars and exotic lifestyles along the way.

Howells, William Dean. *Venetian Life.* 1867. Reprint, Boston: Houghton Mifflin, 1893. In Howells's first travel book he takes pains not to romanticize Venice or to repeat clichés about the famous city. Instead he balances a concern for the city's history with its present-day manners and conventions, although history often dominates.

Howells, William Dean. *Roman Holidays and Others.* New York: Harper & Brothers Publishers, 1908. A late travel book, here Howells is able to offer a lively present-day view of Rome while instructing the reader about its long history. The mixture of the two is more spontaneous here than in his early Venetian book. Roman citizens, especially, come to life.

Howells, William Dean. *Familiar Spanish Travels.* New York: Harper & Brothers Publishers, 1913. With his usual mix of political history, art history, and keen observation of daily life, Howells makes an excellent guide through early twentieth-century Spain. His way of speaking directly to the reader gives Howells a strong narrative presence even today.

Hughes, Langston. *I Wonder as I Wander: An Autobiographical Journey.* New York; Rinehart, 1956. Hughes is ahead of his time here, combining intensely personal recollections with travel scenes, people, and adventures. The time is the politically volatile 1930s; the places are Cuba, Haiti, Russia, Soviet Central Asia, Japan, and Spain.

Huxley, Aldous. *Along the Road: Notes and Essays of a Tourist.* New York: George H. Doran, 1925. A collection of highly opinionated essays of and about travel—everywhere.

Iyer, Pico. *Video Nights in Kathmandu and Other Reports from the Not-So-Far East.* New York: Knopf, 1988. Rambo has infiltrated the exotic East, and Iyer's purpose is to show the anomalies and the traditions that coexist there in the late twentieth century.

James, Henry. *Italian Hours.* Boston: Houghton Mifflin, 1909. Like his novels, James's travel books exhibit a sensitivity to surroundings and a penchant for exquisite prose style.

James, Henry. *The American Scene.* Bloomington: Indiana University Press, 1968. Written after a 20-year absence from America, James's portrait of his own country as a vital, teeming, modern place is both scrupulous and hard. He despairs about the impermanence of America, its materialism, and its new immigrants.

Johnson, Samuel. *A Journey to the Western Islands of Scotland.* 1775. Reprint, New Haven: Yale University Press, 1971. Johnson's version of the well-known tour he and Boswell took together. Johnson's purpose is to experience and understand "quite a different system of life." Unlike Boswell's more gossipy version, Johnson travelogue is concerned with social and political issues almost exclusively.

Kapuściński, Ryszard. *The Emperor.* Translated by William Brand and Katarzyna Mroczkowska-Brand. New York: Vintage Books, 1984. The first book by the little-known but important journalist–travel writer writer from Poland, this book is a series of interviews with what remains of Haile Selassie's court. It is both politically riveting and hilariously absurd.

Kapuściński, Ryszard. *Shah of Shahs.* Translated by William Brand and Katarzyna Mroczkowska-Brand. New York: Harcourt Brace Jovanovich, 1985. Like his book on Ethiopia, this odd travel book explores the uses and abuses of power.

Kapuściński, Ryszard. *The Soccer War.* Translated by William Brand. New York: Knopf, 1991. A collection of essays about the crazy and dangerous world of Central America in the mid-1980s.

Kazantzakis, Nikos. *Russia: A Chronicle of Three Journeys in the Aftermath of the Revolution.* 1956. Reprint, translated by Michael Antonakes and Thanasis Maskalesis, Berkeley: Creative Arts Book Co., 1989. Kazantzakis is interested in social, political, and cultural realities of post-Revolutionary Russia. As always, he is concerned about the level of freedom in peoples' lives. Here he provides a nice balance between travel detail and sociological theory.

Kingsley, Mary. *Travels in West Africa.* 1897. Reprint, Boston: Beacon Press, 1988. An exhaustive study of a relatively small part of Africa.

Kingsley is sympathetic and knowledgeable about native life. The wit with which she manages her escapades is noteworthy.

Krich, John. *Music in Every Room: Around the World in a Bad Mood.* New York: McGraw-Hill, 1984. Marvelously funny, this is another good example of the perpetual dark humor of the post-tourism travel book.

Lawrence, D. H. *Mornings in Mexico.* London: Martin Secker, 1927. This travel book consists of separate sketches written by Lawrence in the mid-1920s when he visited Mexico and the southwestern U.S. He is especially interested in indigenous people in both places.

Lawrence, D. H. *Sea and Sardinia.* New York: T. McBride, 1921. Perhaps Lawrence's best known travel book, it is also his funniest, combining hilarious social comedy with sensitively rendered natural scenes.

Lévi-Strauss, Claude. *Tristes-Tropiques.* 1955. Reprint, translated by John Weightman and Doreen Weightman, London: Jonathan Cape, 1973. Part anthropology, part travel book, this landmark study of the dark side of travel itself may mark the beginning of the post-tourism period.

Mandeville, Sir John. *The Travels of Sir John Mandeville.* c.1356–1357. Reprint, London: Macmillan, 1900. Widely believed now to be a fake travel narrative from the fourteenth century, this book was nonetheless incredibly popular reading up to the eighteenth century.

Matthiessen, Peter. *The Cloud Forest.* New York: Viking Press, 1961. This book describes Matthiessen's largely solitary trip through South America from north to south, between November 1959 and May 1960. Because it is Matthiessen's earliest full-length travel book, it predicts all his later interests: dangerous treks, nature and its misuse, and the loss of primitive societies.

Matthiessen, Peter. *The Snow Leopard.* New York: Viking, 1978. This is the book that made Matthiessen famous as nature-travel writer and soul searcher. A classic of its kind.

Matthiessen, Peter. *African Silences.* New York: Random House, 1991. Less personal than *The Snow Leopard*, this book is about two scientific expeditions the author takes to West and Central Africa, accompanying primatologists and ecologists as is Matthiessen's style of nature-travel.

McPhee, John. *Coming into the Country.* New York: Farrar, Straus, and Giroux, 1977. A very detailed and appealing book about Alaska. McPhee is always a good read because through the naturalistic detail, the people as well as these remote places come alive for the reader.

McPhee, John. *Oranges.* New York: Farrer, Straus, and Giroux, 1966. A classic McPhee combining fascinating detail about the history of the orange with travel adventures in the Florida groves.

Miller, Henry. *The Air Conditioned Nightmare.* New York: New Directions, 1945. The result of a year-long trip through the United States, this book registers Miller's disapproval with mid-century American culture.

Miller, Henry. *The Colossus of Maroussi.* San Francisco: Colt Press, 1941. Here Miller clearly loves everything Greek and is an energetic and opinionated travel guide through Greek towns, ruins, and cafés.

Montagu, Lady Mary Wortley. *Turkish Embassy Letters.* 1763. Reprint, Athens: University of Georgia Press, 1993. Acerbic, sympathetic, and witty, Lady Mary's letters to Alexander Pope and others reveal a sharply observant traveler.

Morris, Jan. *Among the Cities.* New York: Oxford University Press, 1985. A collection of separately written essays about the great cities: Alexandria (1966), Beirut (1956), Chicago (1970), Kashmir (1970), and Manhattan (1979).

Morris, Mary. *Nothing to Declare: Memoirs of Woman Traveling Alone.* New York: Houghton Mifflin, 1988. The story of learning about love, independence, and Mexico.

Murphy, Dervla. *The Waiting Land: A Spell in Nepal.* London: John Murray, 1967. This Irish travel writer goes to Nepal in 1965 to volunteer in the Tibetan refugee camps just across the border. The book is as much about the Tibetans as it is about Nepal.

Naipaul, V. S. *An Area of Darkness.* London: Andre Deutsch, 1964. Naipaul's first travel book and his darkest.

Naipaul, V. S. *India: A Wounded Civilization.* New York: Knopf, 1977. A record of Naipaul's second trip to his ancestral homeland.

Naipaul, V. S. *India: A Million Mutinies Now.* New York: Viking, 1990. Naipaul continues to write about India as a way to understand both it and himself. This book is perhaps his most hopeful.

Naipaul, V. S. *Among the Believers: An Islamic Journey.* London: Andre Deutsch, 1978. As a way to understand Islamic religion and the politics it drives, Naipaul travels from the Middle East to the Far East and offers a lengthy and valuable study of the believers he finds there.

Naipaul, V. S. *Finding the Center.* New York: Alfred A. Knopf, 1984. The most stylistically unusual of Naipaul's travel books, this one explores as much about Naipaul's ideas about writing as it does about West Africa.

Naipaul, V. S. *A Turn in the South.* New York: Knopf, 1989. An unusual venue perhaps for the world traveler–exile, Naipaul turns his attention to race relations in the American South.

Newby, Eric. *Slowly Down the Ganges.* London: Hodder & Stoughton, 1966. In the tradition of British travel writing—witty, urbane, literate—this book takes us 1200 miles down the Ganges River. It also includes color photographs taken by the author.

North , Marianne. *Recollections of a Happy Life.* Edited by Susan Morgan. Charlottesville: University of Pennsylvania Press, 1993. Traveling as a botanical artist through North and South America, the Far East, southern Asia, and Borneo, North's knowledge about the natural world is remarkable.

Polo, Marco. *The Travels of Marco Polo.* c.1299. Reprint, translated by Teresa Waugh, London: Sidgwick & Jackson, 1984. A significant early travel book because it is the first lengthy account of China and the East by a European.

Pritchett, V. S. *At Home and Abroad: Travel Essays.* Berkeley: North Point Press, 1989. A welcome collection of Pritchett's best essays written for magazines. Pritchett is always witty, urbane, and sensitive. In this volume Pritchett includes visits to South America, the United States, Europe, and Canada.

Raban, Jonathan. *Old Glory: An American Voyage.* New York: Simon & Schuster, 1981. British travel writer noted for acerbic and ironic portraits of rural America, Raban ventures in this book to America's heartland—down the Mississippi.

Ralegh, Sir Walter. *The Discoverie of the Large, rich and Beautiful Empyre of Guiana.* . . . 1596. Reprint, edited by V. T. Harlow, London: Argonaut Press, 1928. A popular travel account in the Renaissance, Ralegh's search for El Dorado in South America is mostly about the author as hero.

Rushdie, Salman. *The Jaguar Smile: Nicaraguan Journey.* New York: Viking, 1987. One of the best political-travel accounts about Central America, Rushdie's strengths are his ear for dialogue and his sympathy for the oppressed.

Shoumatoff, Alex. *Florida Ramble.* New York: Harper & Row, 1974. Like McPhee, Shoumatoff is a learned traveling companion whose travels are an excuse to learn more. One of the best books about Florida.

Shoumatoff, Alex. *In Southern Light: Trekking through Zaire and the Amazon.* New York, Knopf, 1986. These two trips combined in one book are more adventurous than Shoumatoff's North American travel books, but their author is nonetheless informed and curious about everything.

Smith, Capt. John. *The True Travels, Adventures, and Observations of Capt. John Smith.* 1630. Reprint, London: T. Slater. An often exciting account of a late-Renaissance traveler-adventurer before he meets Pocahontas.

Smollett, Tobias. *Travels through France and Italy.* 1766. Reprint, Oxford: Clarendon Press, 1979. A grumpy account of un-British-like behavior on the Continent, it is also full of anecdote and wit.

Stark, Freya. *East Is West.* 1945. Reprint, London: Century, 1986. Asked by the Ministry of Information to help the British Government better secure the Middle East during World War II, Stark traveled to the region as a diplomatic consultant. In the book, she is as politically savvy as she is sensitive to the many influences of east on west.

Stark, Freya. *Traveller's Prelude*. London: John Murray, 1950. An intensely personal book by one of the most lyrical travel writers, this fascinating volume—part biography, part travel book—offers insight into an unusually mobile Victorian family. It is indeed a great prelude to many of Stark's many other works.

Steinbeck, John and Robert Capa. *A Russian Journal*. New York: Viking, 1948. An outstanding collaborative travel book about Stalinist Russia in the tradition of Agee and Evans, written and photographed with sympathy for the common Russian citizen.

Steinbeck, John. *Travels with Charley: In Search of America*. 1962. Reprint, Bantam Books, 1963. Accompanied by his dog, Charley, Steinbeck journeys through the United States and delivers an honest appraisal of his homeland and of travel itself.

Stephens, John L. *Incidents of Travel in Yucatan*. New York: Harper & Bros., 1841. One of the early books about eastern Mexico, it has become a classic study of the Mayan culture for its wealth of detail.

Sterne, Laurence. *A Sentimental Journey through France and Italy*. 1768. Reprint, Berkeley: University of California Press, 1967. A thinly veiled fictitious account of Sterne/Yorick's travels on the continent in response to Smollett's grumpier version.

Stevenson, Robert Louis. *Travels with a Donkey in the Cevennes*. London: Chatto & Windus, 1922. A short but exquisite travel piece, full of witty encounters in the south of France.

Theroux, Paul. *The Great Railway Bazaar: By Train through Asia*. Boston: Houghton Mifflin, 1975. A lover of train journeys, Theroux displays in this book his familiar style: aggressive, angry, and witty. He is especially adept at rendering conversation.

Theroux, Paul. *The Old Patagonian Express: By Train through the Americas*. Boston: Houghton Mifflin, 1979. Theroux accomplishes the unlikely plan of taking a train from Boston to Patagonia and meets along the way poets and peasants, but none make him any more content with the vagaries of the developing world.

Thoreau, Henry David. *A Week on the Concord and Merrimack Rivers*. 1849. Reprint, Princeton: Princeton University Press, 1980. As in *Walden,* Thoreau's travels are also journeys into the mind of the author, full of philosophical digressions as well as accounts of the trip.

Thubron, Colin. *Where Nights Are Longest: Travels by Car through Western Russia*. New York: Random House, 1984. Curious about the country he has long feared, Thubron takes a driving-camping trip through western Russia. Thubron is good at dialogue, so the book becomes a lively exchange of ideas.

Tristan, Flora. *Peregrinations of a Pariah*. Translated by Jean Hawkes. Boston: Beacon Press, 1987. Based on her travel diaries from 1833 to 1834, this book is an early example of "conscientious travel." A leading social critic of her day, Tristan travels from Paris to Peru and turns her social concerns to the marginalized—the poor, the indigenous, and women.

Trollope, Francis. *The Domestic Manners of the Americans.* London: Whattaker, Treacher, & Co., 1832. Widely read by many, but hated by Americans in the mid–nineteenth century for critical portraits of its culture (or lack thereof).

Walcott, Derek. *The Fortunate Traveler.* New York: Farrer, Straus, and Giroux, 1981. A travel book in verse by the West Indian poet.

Waugh, Evelyn. *Labels: A Mediterranean Journal.* London: Duckworth, 1930. Waugh's account of a "pleasure cruise in 1929" where he spends more time with other upper-class British than he does with the inhabitants of the ports of call.

Waugh, Evelyn. *Ninety-Two Days: The Account of a Tropical Journey through British Guiana and Part of Brazil.* London: Duckworth, 1943. A more rigorous journey than the one described in *Labels,* this book contains a classic example of "the worst day."

West, Rebecca. *Black Lamb and Grey Falcon: A Journey through Yugoslavia.* London: Macmillan, 1941. A classic travel-political-historical and considered West's best, this book chronicles a 1937 trip through Yugoslavia, but its 1,000 pages tell so much more about the background of this place of ancient animosities.

# Index

Aboriginal, Austrailian, 104–5; dreamings of, 103; songlines of, 103

Adams, Percy G., 123, 127; *Travelers and Travel Liars: 1600–1800*, 123; *Travel Literature and the Evolution of the Novel*, 127

Addison, Joseph, 32

Allen, Alexandra, 124; *Travelling Ladies*, 125

anthropology, 129

Auden, W. H., 19, 62

authenticity: in Beat travel writing, 24–25, 110; in Chatwin, 97; insisting on, 111; in Kingsley, 56; of native groups in travel writing and museum collecting, 128; search for, 23

autobiographical discourse, 58

autobiographical travel books, 4, 14

autobiography, 123, 29, 16; in Naipaul, 83, 91

Bakhtin, Mikhail, 124

Barthes, Roland, 109–10, 124; *Empire of Signs*, 109

Bartram, William, 16, 19, 67, 72; *Travels through North and South Carolina, Georgia, East and West Florida . . .*, 17, 19

Batten, Charles, 123; *Pleasurable Instruction: Form and Convention in Eighteenth-Century Travel Literature*, 123

Baudelaire, Charles, 105

Bell, Gertrude, 2, 44–47, 57–58; *Syria: The Desert and the Sown*, 45

Bird, Isabella, xii, 45–46, 58, 124

Birkett, Dea, 47, 55, 125; *Spinsters Abroad: Victorian Lady Explorers*, 47, 125

Boswell, James, xii, 14–15, 30–43, 50, 70, 72, 81, 124; narrative strategy in, 33; as narrator, 41; political themes in, 31, 32, 35, 38, 40, 42; religious themes in, 31, 35, 38–40, 42; sexual themes in, 31, 32, 35, 37, 39–40, 42; *Account of*

Penrose, Boise, 121; *Travel and Discovery in the Renaissance,* 121
Picasso, Pablo, 21
Plimpton, George, 102
Poe, Edgar Allan, 102
Polo, Marco, 2, 7–9, 121; *Travels,* 7–9
Pope, Alexander, 15, 31; *The Dunciad,* 15
Porter, Dennis, 16, 30, 106, 109, 124; *Haunted Journeys: Desire and Transgression in European Travel Writing,* 106, 124
postcolonial, xiii, 83, 91
postmodernism, xiv, 26
post-tourism, xii, 25–26, 29; in Naipaul, 91
Pratt, Mary Louise, 12, 71, 106, 108–9, 129–31; "Field Work in Common Places," 129; *Imperial Eyes: Travel Writing and Transculturation,* 12, 108, 130
"pretravel," 4, 5
psychological journey, in Greene, 69
psychological travel, xiii, 62

quest, 3, 9–10, 18, 24, 29, 72, 127; in Chatwin, 98, 103; in Matthiessen, 75, 79; scientific, 81

Raban, Jonathan, xiii, 58, 126
Ralegh, Sir Walter, 9–11, 13, 30, 120–21
Renaissance travel, 4
representation, 12, 107
Rilke, Rainer Maria, 104; "Third Sonnet to Orpheus," 104
Rimbaud, Arthur, 105
Rousseau, Jean-Jacques, 3, 16, 32, 34, 36–37, 39
Royal Geographic Society, 45
Russell, Mary, 124; *The Blessings of a Good Thick Skirt,* 124

Said, Edward, 107; *Orientalism,* 109; "Representing the Colonized," 107
Schaller, George, 73–74, 78

science, 111; in Chatwin, 98–99; in travel writing, 15, 71–73
Selassie, Haile, 22
self, xi, xii, 5; discovery of, 15; escape from in Kingsley, 51. *See also* self and world; world
self-reflexivity, 27, 63
self and world (self and other): in Campbell, Mary B., 121; in Chatwin, 97; collapsing distance between, 112; in contemporary travel writing, 26–27; in eighteenth-century travel writing, 11–12; in modern period, 21–22; in Naipaul, 83; in nineteenth-century American travel writing, 18–19; in romantic period, 16; in travel writing, 29, 106, 108. *See also* others; self
sentiment, in travel writing, 15, 71
sentimental, 19
Shakespeare, William, 102, 127
Sheldon, May French, 124
Smollett, Tobias, 14; *Travels Through France and Italy,* 14
Spengemann, William C., 11, 19; *The Adventurous Muse: The Poetics of American Fiction,* 19
Stark, Freya, xiii
Stendhal, 124
Sterne, Laurence, 14; *A Sentimental Journey,* 14
Stevenson, Catherine Barnes, 125; *Victorian Women Travelers in Africa,* 125
Stevenson, Robert Louis, xii, 19
Stout, Janis, 3
Strabo, 1; *Geographica,* 1
Sundance Kid, 99–100
Swift, Jonathan, 15; *Gulliver's Travels,* 15

Taylor, Annie, 124
Theroux, Paul, 102, 108–9, 126; *The Old Patagonian Express,* 108
Thoreau, Henry David, xi, 17; *A Week on the Concord and Merrimack Rivers,* 19